The Construction
of the History of Religion
in Schelling's Positive Philosophy

The Construction of the History of Religion in Schelling's Positive Philosophy

Its Presuppositions and Principles

Paul Tillich

Translated with an Introduction and Notes by
Victor Nuovo

Lewisburg
Bucknell University Press
London: Associated University Presses

Associated University Presses, Inc.
Cranbury, New Jersey 08512

Associated University Presses
108 New Bond Street
London W1Y OQX, England

Library of Congress Cataloging in Publication Data

Tillich, Paul, 1886–1965.
The construction of the history of religion in Schelling's positive philosophy.

Translation of Die religiongeschichtliche Konstruktion in Schellings positiver Philosophie.
Originally presented as the author's thesis, Breslau, 1910.
Includes bibliographical references.
1. Schelling, Friedrich Wilhelm Joseph von, 1775–1854. 2. Religion—History. I. Title.
B2899.R4T5413   193   73–22865
ISBN 0-8387-1422-6

PRINTED IN THE UNITED STATES OF AMERICA

CONTENTS

PREFACE

The present work is a translation of Tillich's earliest work, *Die religionsgeschichtliche Konstruktion in Schellings positiver Philosophie,* his philosophical doctoral dissertation presented at the University of Breslau and published by H. Fleischmann Verlag in 1910. The translation is complete. Tillich's longer notes have been put at the end of the work; citations have been put in parentheses in the text. Quotations from Schelling's works are cited by volume and page according to the standard edition (F. W. J. von Schelling, *Sämtliche Werke,* edited by K. F. A. Schelling, Stuttgart, 1856–61). I follow Manfred Schröter's practice of numbering the volumes of this edition consecutively (1–14) instead of according to the two divisions of the standard edition (1, 1–9; 2, 1–4). I have checked all of Tillich's citations of Schelling and have made corrections where necessary. Where I have been unable to locate a quotation in Schelling's work, I have indicated this by *sic* after the references given by Tillich. Superscript arabic numerals in the text refer to Tillich's notes; they are numbered consecutively throughout each part of the work. Superscript lower-case roman numerals refer to the translator's notes.

Translations from Schelling's works are my own. I have, however, consulted the following translations: Albert Hofstadter, *System of Transcendental Idealism* (selections in *Philosophies of Art and Beauty*, edited by Hofstadter and Kuhns, New York, 1964); E. S. Morgan, *On University Studies* (thoroughly revised by Norbert Guterman, Athens, Ohio, 1966); James Gutmann, *Of Human Freedom* (Chicago, 1936); F. deW. Bolman, *The Ages of the World* (New York, 1942). In a few instances I have borrowed from these translations; in every case this is indicated by the translator's name.

I am grateful to Middlebury College for several grants awarded me from the Faculty Research Fund while I was engaged in translating, writing, and revising this work. Others, colleagues and friends, have aided and supported me in numerous ways, and I take great pleasure in acknowledging their assistance here. My colleague Robert Ferm was the first to suggest that this translation, which I began for my students' use, should be published. My colleagues in the Department of Philosophy, Stanley Bates and Mark Temin, enlightened me on numerous philosophical points; both of them read an early version of my introduction and provided valued criticism. Robert Hill, of the Department of English, also read an early version of my introduction; his criticisms were devastating and, I hope, carefully followed in the revisions made. Barbara Madison typed the manuscript and corrected my errors. During the last stages of this work, I have been the grateful recipient of sound criticism and good advice from my editor, Mathilde E. Finch, who is also a fellow Hegelian. James Luther Adams has been a help to me at every step of the way. I did not know him before I began this work, yet ever since I first wrote him about Tillich, he has responded in abundance with good advice and encouragement and friendship. My wife has not read the manuscript or my thoughts (about

Tillich), yet she has supported me in ways that I cannot and should not mention here. Life and freedom we have sought together and shared.

Victor Nuovo

Middlebury, Vermont

TRANSLATOR'S INTRODUCTION

I recall the unforgettable moment when by chance I came into possession of the very rare first edition of the collected works of Schelling in a bookstore on my way to the University of Berlin. I had no money, but I bought it anyway, and this spending of nonexistent money was probably more important than all the other nonexistent or sometimes existing money that I have spent. For what I learned from Schelling became determinative of my own philosophical and theological development.[1]

—Paul Tillich

That Tillich is indebted to Schelling in a fundamental way is well known, for he has acknowledged it often and emphatically. But, although that debt has been recorded in detail in Tillich's two earliest works, few have had the opportunity to measure its nature and extent. The first work, Tillich's philosophical dissertation, was never reprinted; the second, his theological dissertation, reappeared only in 1959 in the first volume of Tillich's collected works in German.[2] Only a few detailed studies of them have been made,

1. Paul Tillich, *Perspectives on 19th and 20th Century Protestant Theology* (New York, 1967), p. 142.
2. Tillich's second Schelling dissertation, *Mystik und Schuldbewusstsein in Schellings philosophischer Entwicklung,* was presented at Halle and published in 1912 by

11

and these remain unpublished.[3] Tillich's dissertations appear now, for the first time in an English translation, over sixty years after their original publication.[4] During these years, Tillich left Germany as a political exile and came to the United States where he became a leading figure in American theology. He was nearly fifty years old when he came to America; the foundations of his thought were securely laid, and its structure virtually complete.

The importance of Tillich's Schelling dissertations for understanding his thought cannot be emphasized enough. They are not peripheral works, nor are they mere *Jugendschriften*, youthful works that throw light on a great thinker's development but must remain subordinate to later definitive works (for example, in the case of Hegel and Marx). On the contrary, these works provide the vital link with Tillich's intellectual and spiritual heritage. They reveal the first formulation of the method and system from which he never departed and the principal themes with which he was concerned throughout his career. It is as though the principles of Schelling's later philosophy, as they are presented by Tillich in these early works, found a place at the very roots of his consciousness and determined all his future thought. I shall argue later in this introduction that Tillich's dissertations reveal the "deep structure" of his thought, which may be likened to a "language" with which one "speaks" about existence.

C. *Bertelsmann Verlag.* It is reprinted in the first volume of Tillich's Gesammelte Werke, *Frühe Hauptwerke* (Stuttgart, 1959).
   3. Three dissertations have been written in English on Tillich's Schelling dissertations; all, as yet, are unpublished: Daniel J. O'Hanlon, *The Influence of Schelling on the Thought of Paul Tillich* (Rome, Pontifical Gregorian University, 1957); Guenther Friedrich Sommer, *The Significance of the Late Philosophy of Schelling for the Formation and Interpretation of the Thought of Paul Tillich* (Duke University, 1960); Harold H. Zietlow, *The Living God: the Existential Systems of F. W. J. Schelling and Paul Tillich* (University of Chicago, 1964).
   4. For an English translation of Tillich's second Schelling dissertation, cf. Paul Tillich, *Mysticism and Guilt-Consciousness in Schelling's Philosophical Development,* Translated with an Introduction and Notes by Victor Nuovo (Cranbury, N.J., 1974).

Tillich's thought is an outgrowth of classical German philosophy. Even his theological formulations are mediated through this tradition. Classical German philosophy begins with Kant's critical philosophy and can be said to be a systematic pursuit of solutions to problems that are caused by the dualities arising within the critical philosophy and that were apparently left unsolved by Kant himself: the duality of thought and reality, of the subjective and the objective, of practical and theoretical reason, of freedom and nature, and so forth. Tillich's dissertations may be viewed as attempts, through Schellingian concepts, to overcome the Kantian antithesis of historical faith and moral religion, and to provide a metaphysical basis for Kant's doctrine of radical evil and the self-estrangement of the autonomous moral will. Solutions to these antagonisms were sought through systematic constructions that deduce the manifold of being and its essential distinctions from the unity of the absolute. Hence the study of classical German philosophy is properly a study of systems rather than of problems, because problems have their solution only when they are viewed as parts of the whole.

The study of Schelling's philosophy is complicated by the fact that Schelling developed not one but apparently several systems during the course of his long career. Therefore, the task of Schelling scholarship is to identify these systems and their principles, and further, on the assumption that the total product of Schelling's philosophical activity possesses intrinsic unity, to present them as successive periods or stages of development. Each stage is a system or totality, and totalities produce other totalities, not in a linear but in a dialectical way. Philosophical perplexities arise from inconsistencies within one stage or system that cannot be contained by it and that cause its overthrow or catastrophe and thereby, through postulation and demand, initiate the transition to a higher synthesis. The perplexities or questions of the preceding system are answered in the one that follows. The method that Tillich follows in his second Schelling dissertation is a variation of this dialectical method; it reappears in his later work as the "method of correlation."

Recent Schelling scholarship has argued in favor of Schelling's late philosophy (the philosophy of mythology and revelation) as the culmination of his philosophical development, rather than his system of identity, favored by earlier scholarship.[5] This is precisely the emphasis given in Tillich's Schelling dissertations. Hence, although written over sixty years ago, these works may serve the English reader as introductions to Schelling scholarship. Of course, I must hasten to add that Schelling scholarship has surpassed Tillich's early formulations; yet it is not unreasonable to hope that the study of Tillich's dissertations may call forth additional translations of works by and about Schelling (for there is little now in English of either kind), and evoke original studies in English of Schelling's late philosophy. For Schelling is important in his own right. Surely at a time when there seems to be a significant increase of interest in Hegel, Schelling's criticism of Hegel's philosophy must not be overlooked. Yet not only as a critic of Hegel is Schelling important. If Schelling is not the greatest philosopher of his age, he is surely its most representative. During sixty years of philosophical activity, he lived through all the essential moments of German thought and intellectual life, so that it is not unreasonable to claim that German philosophy met its fate in him. To neglect him is to deprive this tradition of some of its richest content. Furthermore, Schelling's late philosophy, when viewed in

5. W. Schulz, s. v. Schelling, in *Die Religion im Geschichte und Gegenwart,* 3d ed. (Tübingen, 1957). See also below, translator's note i, for a discussion of recent Schelling scholarship.

retrospect, seems to anticipate more or less recent developments in philosophy and theology: his concepts of monotheism and revelation suggest Barth; on the other hand, modern philosophical theism or panentheism bears the marks of his influence, as do existentialism, the comparative study of mythology, and the history of religions. Tillich's explication of Schelling's thought in both dissertations is based upon Schelling's doctrine of being, his doctrine of the potencies. Tillich's most complete account of this doctrine is given in Part I of his first dissertation: Part I,I,1 presents the development of the doctrine in Schelling's thought prior to his late philosophy; Part I,I,2 presents the doctrine in its final form in Schelling's late or "positive" philosophy (the reader who finds Tillich's rapid survey in the first section confusing may be well advised to begin reading here); in Part I, II, Tillich develops Schelling's doctrines of God, the world, and man in the light of his doctrine of the potencies. Whereas Part I, I presents the basic system of Schelling's philosophy, Part I, II presents its "scenario," for the potencies are the principles of a living process of self-realization, whether the subject of this process be God, the world, or man. In this process, the person realizes itself by overcoming the contradiction of original principles that lie within it. In what follows, I shall present a brief account of the doctrine of the potencies based in part on Tillich's presentation and in part on my own reading of Schelling. It is not meant to be definitive, but only to clarify the doctrine that became the underlying structure of Tillich's thought.

The potencies (German: *Potenz,* Latin: *potentia,* Greek: δύναμις) define what is *(das Seiende).* They are protean concepts that contain a richness of content drawn from the history of religion and philosophy and even more basically from sources that seem to be as old as consciousness itself.

They are the highest metaphysical concepts, comprehending both the operations of nature and the actions of freedom. "It is fortunate," said Schelling in his lectures on the philosophy of revelation, "that the highest speculative concepts are always at the same time the deepest moral concepts, which are close to everyone" (SW, 13:67). There are three potencies. The first two, theoretically considered, constitute the possibility of the original contradiction of being. The first potency is the ground or basis of all that is. It is the material cause, substance, the principle of individuation, of *real* objectivity that resists thought. In Schelling's system this principle is reinterpreted as the irrational will to selfhood. It is desire, that which is not, that longs to be something. The first potency is nonbeing, μὴ ὄν, that which can be but is not, which, by a self-positing act, becomes what is but ought not to be. It is the negation of essential being and the unconscious ground of personality. The first potency is also the real or sacramental basis of religion, the holy in its most primitive manifestation, the demonic or heteronomous force that gains objectivity for itself but resists true universality. The second potency is the formal and efficient cause of being. It is that which is, pure and simple, pure being, the original content of thought. As pure act, it struggles to become the universal potency of being, but it can become such only by overcoming the first potency. The second potency is complete selflessness. It is the principle of love, which subjects itself to the negation of the first principle, the negation of universality by particularity, in order to overcome it. As the principle of limitation, so that it may check the otherwise limitless force of the first potency, it causes the existence of the manifold, and joins itself to this manifold, but only ideally and externally. Hence, tragically, it becomes the principle of finitude, necessary being. Everything that exists, exists through the interaction of the first and the second potencies, and hence is destined to the futility of death and decay as regards its particular substance, or to abstract universality as regards its form. The second potency is autonomous will, practical reason, the cause of conscious life and personality. In the history of religion, Christ is the supreme manifestation of the second potency, who struggles against the dominion of the first potency and subjects himself to its wrath. This act of self-surrender is wholly moral and thereby becomes the norm of true universality in all religion. The Christ is also the bearer of the third potency, spirit, the final cause. Spirit is the unity of the first and second potencies. As actuality or entelechy, it is the self-possessing cause that does not lose itself, because it posits everything harmoniously within itself. Hence it includes both the formal and material causes, and is self-moved. It is the perfect, the living whole, the unity of the real and the ideal, the concrete universal. In the realm of nature, spirit is the organic; in the realm of art, it is the unity of the conscious and the unconscious in every creative act; in the personality, it is the unity of drives, uniting the will to selfhood and the will to love, freedom and autonomy. In philosophy, spirit is the unity of theoretical and practical reason, of reason and history. Spirit is νοῦς, mind or intellect, but in addition to the clarity of intellect, it possesses the fullness and concreteness of life. The age of the spirit is the age of universal history, an age that unites the particular and the universal, the concrete historical and the moral. Spirit is the principle of hope, of what ought to be and shall be *(das sein Sollende)*.

God and man are both spirit. God is the indissoluble unity of the potencies, the eternally living one. The potencies, then, constitute the trinitarian nature of God. As the absolute, God is the culmination of speculative thought. He is "being itself," "that which is what is" (*das was das Seiende ist* - τὸ τὶ ἦν εἶναι), the indissoluble substance or subject of being, the *that* which is. As person, God is beyond being (*das Überseiende*): God is free from his being, free to be what he will be. He is free to reveal himself out of the future as the goal that thought, limited to what is, cannot anticipate. Within the being of God the world in its ideality is formed together with the first man. This world has its center, its inwardness, in this ideal man, for in man the potencies have a spiritual equilibrium, and man, like God, is free from them. On account of this equilibrium, the world exists beside God (*praeter deum*), but in immediate relationship with him. Man, the living soul, is the link between God and the world. In him resides the possibility of their separation.

At this point it is well to remind ourselves that Schelling's thought was, in all of its periods, speculative, and that the aim of speculative thought is to explain the origin of the manifold from the one absolute being. This was not Tillich's purpose, either in his dissertations or in his later works. His philosophical orientation was consistently critical rather than speculative. His concept of critical philosophy was broad enough to include ontology, but Tillich's ontology is not a speculative metaphysics. However, traces of this speculative theology and cosmogony remain in Tillich's thought, and this is especially so with respect to the doctrine of the Fall. It is by means of the doctrine of the Fall that Schelling explained the origin of the external manifold and of the human race, of nature and history. His doctrine is a composite of Original Sin and the Platonic fall, although neither retains its original meaning. Following Kant, Schelling insisted that sin must not be construed as a moral deficiency, but as a transcendental spiritual act, as radical evil. By an original free act, the first man, who continues to live in us all, sets (posits) himself and the world outside God *(extra deum)*. The ground or origin of this act resides in God, but in "that within God which is not God himself"; it resides in the unconscious ground, the will to selfhood, the first potency. On account of the Fall, the first man becomes the father of men; the world ceases to be the world in truth, a cosmos of internal order and harmony. Now the world has become an aggregate of separate things, a sequence of haphazard events and conflicting principles, without any intrinsic order and without a center. The children of the first man wander within this world until they die. In estrangement, man asks questions about himself, and, because of what he once was, these questions are also about being and God; man is the question of being whose answer is God. This original act of self-assertion is the supra-historical beginning of existence and has both ontological and moral significance: ontologically it is the beginning of existence, morally it is the first sin. This speculative scheme is the basis of Tillich's concept of existence.

In the introduction to his first Schelling dissertation, Tillich described the task of the work as follows: "to present the construction of the history of religion as the focal point of Schelling's positive philosophy." The construction itself is set forth in Part II of the dissertation. The purpose of the construction, however, is to provide material for the development of the twin concepts of religion and history in Part III of the dissertation. The formulation of these concepts is, according to Tillich, "the systematic task of the present." Tillich is quite correct in making the history of religion the focal point of Schelling's positive philosophy, for it is precisely history that constitutes the positivity of philosophy and religion that reveals history's inmost meaning. Positive philosophy is the hermeneutics of historical events and traditions viewed as moments in a process that culminates in revelation. However, the hermeneutical principles of positive philosophy are the potencies, which we come to know through metaphysical reflection, through pure thought. Therefore, positive philosophy must rely upon the complementary activity of negative philosophy, namely, the theory of purely rational first principles. "Positive philosophy," therefore, is not an adequate title for Schelling's late philosophy.

The presupposition of history is the Fall. The consequence of the Fall is the separation of the potencies. The potencies viewed as moments of self-realization no longer have the simultaneity of moments of an eternal process; rather, they have become separated in time. The potencies are now signs of past, present, and future. The goal is no longer immediately present, but hidden in the future. The task of positive philosophy is so to construct the history of religion as to point to history's hidden or esoteric meaning. That history's meaning should be religious is due to the essence of man: in every act, moral or aesthetic, that gives meaning to human existence, man posits God and at the same time makes history. Human consciousness is "God-positing consciousness." Man's relationship to God as the ground of his existence can never be dissolved (if it could, man would cease to be anything at all); but it can be distorted. History, then, is the history of errors, but errors that anticipate truth. History is the process through which consciousness overcomes its original act of existential self-assertion and looks to a higher unity with God than that which it first had. History is an ethico-religious process. However, the goal of history is not within the capacity of human consciousness to deduce or produce, for the goal is the absolute freedom of God from his being, the freedom of God to be all in all. Hence, revelation is a necessary postulate of positive philosophy.

In the introductory lecture to the second book of his *Philosophy of Revelation*, Schelling presents a brief outline of his concept of religion (SW, 13:189ff.). Schelling's outline treats in general the same themes that Tillich discusses in the second and third parts of his first dissertation. I offer a brief account of it here, because it focuses on the concept of "philosophical religion," which receives adequate emphasis in neither of Tillich's dissertations. For Schelling, philosophical religion is the culmination of the historical construction of religion; for Tillich, in the dissertations, it is an afterthought. Yet, as an ideal, philosophical religion remains operative in Tillich's later works.

Schelling's construction is an attempt primarily to distinguish between rational religion *(Vernunftreligion)* and philosophical religion *(philosophische Religion)*. At the outset, he divides religion into two classes: scientific religion *(wissenschaftliche Religion)* and unscientific religion. Scientific religion is pure rational religion; its principle is the original unity of the intellect and its object. It is thoroughly ideal and unhistorical. Elsewhere (SW, 11:569) Schelling says that it is not religion at all. He defines it so that it may be rejected. In contrast to it, unscientific religion is based upon a real relationship of consciousness to God that antecedes reason and undergoes a real historical development through three principal forms: mythology, revelation, and philosophical religion, which Schelling also calls "the religion of free philosophical knowledge." Philosophical knowledge is to be distinguished from rational knowledge: the former is the more comprehensive term including, besides knowledge of pure rational principles, knowledge of positive historical facts.[6] It should be noted in passing that this distinction is basic to the theme of Tillich's second dissertation; his definitions of mysticism and guilt-consciousness are dependent upon it.

6. Schelling's conception of positive historical facts includes a dimension not ordinarily attributed to empirical events. The historical events that are intended here are of a "higher" type that includes events in the divine as well as in human life; cf. SW 13:195.

In mythology, or paganism, consciousness posits a sequence of gods. They are false gods, but not entirely so, for they are expressions of consciousness's original relationship to God through the first potency. In mythology, God is represented as though he were beside himself, outside his divinity; he is represented as nature, as pure elemental life, as wrath. Revelation presupposes mythology, not in a merely logical sense, but in a personal developmental sense; mythology is the real process that must precede the stage of revelation. Mythology is natural religion, revelation is supernatural religion; supernatural is not the negation of the natural, not the unnatural, but the correlate of the natural. In revelation, God is revealed to consciousness in the unity of his potencies, in the fullness of his being and in his freedom from it. On the basis of a real relationship with God, a relationship that antecedes thought, and through the conquest of this relationship, consciousness is able to enter into a free and personal relationship with the living God, who is the lord of being. This divine-human relationship is made possible through the agency of the second potency, the Son, who is incarnate as the Christ. Philosophical religion is Idealism, refounded by Schelling upon the original realism of mythology and the spiritual realization of Christianity. It is, in terms of the potencies, the expression of the age of the Spirit. It is free thought and cognition, which are not limited by the externality and separateness of things; it is the organon of spiritual knowledge, of the true end of all things. It is "futurology." But it is a form of spiritual life that cannot be attained except by those who undergo the real process of redemption mediated by mythology and revelation. Finally, it should be noted that in this same lecture Schelling distinguishes between two aspects of history, the esoteric and the exoteric: the former is religion, the latter is the state. Both are forms of life whose goal is freedom. The state cannot exist apart from religion, which sanctifies it. Yet the religious sanctification of the state is not meant to conserve existing regimes (although this was the case with Olympian religion); like the Greek mysteries and Hebrew prophetism, religion is the source of radical utopian visions. Although Tillich does not develop this theme in his dissertations, it may indeed be that here we have the seed of his social theory of history, of the *kairos*, of his theory of religious socialism.

In all his works, Tillich displays a remarkable continuity of thought. In striking contrast to Schelling, his thought underwent no radical transformation. It emerged fully developed in all of its essential characteristics at the beginning of his career. The abiding deep structure of Tillich's thought is the system of the potencies. Wherever one looks in Tillich's works he will encounter them. Yet in Tillich's hands they are no longer the speculative principles that they once were in Schelling; they have become more method than metaphysics. In the same way, Tillich seems to have stopped short of Schelling's goal of philosophical religion in favor of a systematic theology that is primarily apologetic. Indeed, in contrast to Schelling, who was always more concerned with the definition of principles than with their use, Tillich appears to be a structuralist rather than a metaphysician. By structuralism I mean an aprioristic, nonspeculative systematics whose purpose is interpretation and whose principles are neither forms nor contents, but the essential elements of things and their relationships. This systematic method is not inconsistent with Schelling's conception of positive philosophy, although it significantly reduces its speculative power.

In his *Systematic Theology*, the potencies appear as the principles of Tillich's doctrine of being: in the self-world polarity, and the further elaboration of this polarity in the concepts of individuality, dynamics, and freedom on the one hand, and of participation, form, and destiny on the other (ST, 1: 169–86). This basic polarity is the opposition of the first and second potencies, and the possibility of their unity is unambiguous life, or spirit. Because they are separable, the potencies become the "structure of destruction" or of estrangement (ST, 2:60f.). The same scenario of freedom and redemption applies to Tillich's ontological elements as applies to the potencies: freedom becomes aroused and departs from essence and its immediate unity with God. Freedom then becomes arbitrariness, and destiny becomes fate or necessity; dynamics (potency) becomes aimlessness and chaos, form becomes external law; the individual cannot participate in objective structures without fear of self-loss; he is overcome by doubt and loneliness (ST, 2: 62–66). Through the mediation of the Christ (the incarnation of the second potency), the New Being becomes a real possibility (in contrast to the ideal possibility of essential being); New Being is more than the restoration of essential being; it is the conquest of estrangement through a real process of regeneration, justification, and sanctification, that is, through the spiritual life (ST, 2:165ff.; 3:138ff.). New Being presupposes, that is, must be preceded by, estrangement (the necessity implied here is for Tillich not teleological); it presupposes a real although distorted relationship to God as the ground of being mediated through the freedom of the first potency, a relationship that antecedes thought, and the conquest of this distortion through faith and courage in spite of estrangement. The process of redemption, therefore, must be positive and historical, and must proceed by way of life and history interpreted respectively in the light of their goals of Spirit and the Kingdom under the inspiration of those fateful moments, *kairoi,* when estrangement is conquered and the goal anticipated. The anticipated goal is the unity of being that is realized by Absolute Freedom (God) from being itself, by supernatural grace. It is this structure and scenario, then, that give shape and meaning to the very rich content of Tillich's *Systematic Theology*.

I shall give only a few brief additional examples to illustrate the continuing presence of the potencies in Tillich's formulations. The triadic concepts of power, justice, and love, and of heteronomy (original theonomy—the real or sacramental religious relationship that antecedes thought), autonomy, and theonomy apply the potencies to various cultural realizations: artistic, political, religious. Ultimate concern, Tillich's definition of religion, presupposes the system of the potencies (ST, 1:211): the emphasis on concreteness and ultimacy emphasizes the positivity of religion and its ground in a relationship mediated by the first potency (which in its separateness is experienced as wrath and the terror of the demonic), a relationship that thought cannot anticipate or surpass (the original religious relationship is real and not ideal; only on the basis of this real relationship can the ultimate of speculative reason be identified with the religious ultimate); this religious relationship is humanized throughout history, assaulted and condemned by the second potency in its quest for the spiritual ultimate that will set it free.

Thus far, I have argued that the essential structure of Tillich's thought had been realized in his early studies of Schelling's late philosophy and have attempted to show that this structure is the same as his construction of Schelling's doctrine of the potencies. I have attempted to illustrate the operation of this structure in Tillich's later works. I have also argued that in making Schelling's thought his own, Tillich stopped short of Schelling's goal of philosophical religion. I must now qualify this claim by noting that, although Tillich did not explicitly advocate the goal of philosophical religion, it is present in his work as an implicit goal: for example, Tillich's *Systematic Theology* is not strictly apologetics; through the method of correlation and the reinterpretation of Christian doctrine by means of philosophical concepts that originate in Idealism and Existentialism, Tillich attempted to free theology from heteronomy and to develop within it an openness to other creative spiritual realizations; he sought to liberate Christian religious consciousness from an external bondage to tradition so that the spiritual and universally human import of its content might be comprehended anew. Even the apologetic concept of "the God above the God of theism"[7] illustrates Tillich's attempt to transcend traditional theology by "filling it full" with radically new spiritual content. Nowhere, however, does this goal of philosophical religion become more explicit than in the writings of Tillich's last years, in which he expressed a concern for a contemporary dialogue of Christian theology and other world religions. I shall consider these writings in the final section of this introduction.

During the last years of his life, Tillich became deeply involved in the question of the relation of Christianity to other historical or universal religions. This question was the theme of his Bampton Lectures, given at Columbia University in 1961 and published in 1963 under the title of *Christianity and the Encounter of World Religions.* In the opinion of Mircea Eliade, this book—especially its third chapter, which presents the outline of a dialogue with Buddhism— marks "the beginning of a new phase in Paul Tillich's thought."[8] In 1963, Tillich went from Harvard to the University of Chicago, and during the winter and autumn

7. Paul Tillich, *The Courage to Be* (New Haven, 1952), pp. 186ff.
8. Paul Tillich, *The Future of Religions* (New York, 1966), p. 32.

terms of 1964 participated with Eliade in a seminar on the history of religions and systematic theology. Tillich acknowledged the importance of this joint venture in "The Significance of the History of Religions for the Systematic Theologian,"[9] a public lecture that he delivered only ten days before his death. In this lecture he expressed the need for a more prolonged interaction between systematic theology and the study of the history of religions than hitherto had been the case. He also expressed the hope that the structure of religious thought might develop in connection with another or different fragmentary manifestation of theonomy or of the "Religion of the Concrete Spirit."[10]

What transformation must theology undergo in its encounter with the history of religions, and with the constructive efforts of universal religions in the present age? Tillich does not answer this question, but merely explores its dimensions. In his explorations he returns to the themes of his dissertations: the construction of the history of religion and the apparent anthesis of mysticism and guilt-consciousness.

In the first part of "The Significance of the History of Religions for the Systematic Theologian," Tillich asserts the importance of the history of religions for the theologian and thereby opposes orthodox theologians who reject all religions as false except their own, and secular theologians who reject the real basis of all religions. He contends that religion is a universally human phenomenon that reveals the depth of man's spiritual nature in its historically conditioned situation. Religion is the interaction of sacred substance and critical protest—mystical, prophetic, and secular: mystical protest is the spiritual realization of the theoretical faculty (cf. above, Schelling's concept of *Ver-*

9. Printed in *ibid.*, pp. 80–94.
10. *Ibid.*, p. 91.

nunftreligion); prophetic and secular protest are the spiritual realizations of the practical faculty of reason. In the realm of estrangement, however, they are expressions of the second potency in its struggle against the first (hence Tillich's word *protest).* Secular protest is primarily prophetic protest that has totally repressed the real basis of consciousness. It is consistent Kantianism. The interaction of sacrament and crisis constitutes the revelatory process within history. The history of religions has significance for the theologian so long as it can be viewed in the light of revelatory events, for theology is a normative discipline. Tillich suggests that there *may* be a "central event in the history of religion which unites the positive results of those critical developments in the history of religion in and under which revelatory experiences are going on—an event which, therefore, makes possible a concrete theology that has universalistic significance."[11] He has in mind the "Christ event." It is this event that gives concrete historical substance to critical protest and safeguards it from the onslaughts of a demonic heteronomy. This substance is not the old sacramental substance of the past, but the new liberating substance of the spiritual religion of the future. In the present work, Tillich does not assert the uniqueness of this event, but considers its possibility alongside others. This shift in emphasis is significant.

In the second part of his lecture, Tillich presents his own "dynamic-typological" construction of the history of religions. The principles of the construction are the same as those set forth by him in his first Schelling dissertation: the real basis, critical protest, and spiritual fulfillment, the three potencies. But there is here an important difference: the two forms of critical protest, the mystical and the eth-

11. *Ibid.,* p. 81.

ical, are retained. In the construction presented in Part II of the first dissertation mystical criticism marked the culmination and catastrophe of the mythological period, whereas ethical protest inaugurated the period of revelation. Now they appear side by side in time as equally valid forms of the struggle of the critical principle against the sacramental basis and toward concrete universality. The goal of the history of religions, its inner telos, is the "Religion of the Concrete Spirit," which is the organic unity of the sacramental basis and mystical and ethical criticism. This goal, however, is fully anticipated by no historical religious tradition. By whom is it anticipated? By the theologian. who discerns the goal in terms of the underlying structure of every historical religion, and who, informed by this structure (which is also the universal structure of being and of consciousness), participates through his understanding in the fragmentary realization of the goal that is the substance of every historical religion. To be sure, the theologian is not indifferent to differences and conflicts between historical religions, but he experiences them not as irreconcilable differences, but as aspects of a creative tension or opposition. The theologian, then, becomes the interpreter of a creative pluralism in the history of religions.

Tillich's conversation or dialogue with Buddhism, described rather schematically in the third chapter of *Christianity and the Encounter of the World Religions,* is his only attempt at this method of interpretation. I shall present a critical account of it. A meaningful dialogue between Buddhism and Christianity must be based upon a dynamic typology. A dynamic typology distinguishes between classes of things not in terms of unique characteristics, but in terms of basic elements common to each class. All classes have the same elements; they differ because the elements are polar and are therefore capable of conflict and resolution in which one element becomes dominant in varying degrees. There are three elements common to all historical religions: the sacramental, the mystical, and the ethical. Each of these elements can dominate the others in a polar situation; hence three general types of religion are possible: the sacramental, the mystical, and the ethical. Only the last two are higher religions, because only they have universality. Buddhism is a mystical type of religion; Christianity, an ethical. A dialogue between them is possible because of the elements common to them. The dialogue discusses the capability of each tradition to respond to an immediate sociopolitical task; it asks, which of the two can provide a spiritual basis for secular democracy in contemporary Japan? The key to an answer is the inner spiritual aim, or telos, of each, which is determined by the dominant element in each type. Tillich expresses doubt that Buddhism will be able to provide a spiritual basis for democracy in Japan, because its telos is expressed by the symbol of Nirvana, an ontological symbol of identity. Like all mystical types of religion, Buddhism seeks identity and not community. Buddhist *karuna* is not the same as Christian *agape*. It is not concerned with the transformation of society or the fate of the individual. Christianity, then, seems more responsive to the social task; the symbol of its telos, "the Kingdom of God," embodies these concerns—although this is not the case with every historical form of Christianity. The dialogue is not ended, however. A radical change is possible within Buddhism, a shift in emphasis from the mystical to the ethical principle is possible; indeed it is already taking place.

Tillich's interpretation of Buddhism is clearly in error. Guided by his conception of mysticism as ontological identity—a theoretical rather than an ethical concept—he overlooks not the possibility of the ethical element in Buddhism, but the overwhelming evidence of its actuality.[12] For Buddhism is eminently ethical. Salvation in Buddhism comes only through supreme moral effort by the agent self. It is not the moral self, the person, but the particular substantial self that is negated in Buddhism. Moreover, the possibility for community is greater in Buddhism than in Christianity, for Christianity envisages a community of all humanity—or, at most, of all rational beings—with God. To be sure, they shall dwell together in a new heaven and a new earth. Buddhist social consciousness, however, comprehends all of life in an infinity of worlds; one need only recall the picture of the great Buddhist assemblies in various Mahayana sutras. Nor are individual differences overlooked in Buddhist ethics: the four *Brahmaviharas* are sufficient proof of this; and surely Buddhist canonical literature is not indifferent to social-ethical themes, for instance, the picture of a Buddhist utopia in the larger *Sukhavativyuha Sutra*. It is also not obvious that Buddhism is less historical than Christianity. The Buddha is not a mythical figure, howevermuch his life may be obscured by legend; rather like the Christ, he is an ethico-religious figure: he overcomes existential self-assertion and sacramental religion by moral resolve; he awakens hope (and what is true historical existence but hope mediated by morality?) by revealing the dynamic inner law and goal of existence; he founds a universal community. Indeed, Buddhism and Christianity are structurally the same: their doctrines (and Schelling's claim that doctrine is action applies here) create persons, found universal societies, and initiate historical movements. Both achieve concrete universality in historical communities: both church and sangha are manifestations of spirit. The profound difference between Buddhism and Christianity is

12. Cf., Trevor Ling, "Buddhist Mysticism," *Religious Studies*[1], no. 2 (April 1966).

between the supra-historical goal, or its symbol, that each envisages: Nirvana and Glory. Nirvana must be seen as the goal of history and not its negation.

Tillich's error, then, lies in his conception of mysticism as nonhistorical ontological identity. He has interpreted Buddhism and other Asian religions, as well as neoplatonism and its variants, in terms of this concept. But, perhaps because Schelling was not drawn to this form of mysticism as Tillich was, he did not regard it as an authentic form of historical religion. Of course, Schelling also believed that the goal of historical religion must ultimately be mediated only by Christianity. The goal, philosophical religion, would differ from Christianity only in form, not in spirit. The moral of all of this, and I believe there is one, is that historical religions must be interpreted historically, and not in terms of nonhistorical principles. Christianity is not the only historical religion. Buddhism is another, and there are others. It is to Tillich's credit that he envisaged this plurality in his concept of the "Religion of the Concrete Spirit," although he did not adequately interpret it. In envisaging it, he laid the foundations for a broader conception of Schelling's conception of philosophical religion. The task of this "discipline" will be to clarify the ethical demands of world religions by interpreting them as expressions of hope. Tillich's legacy is the possibility of this turning, in his thought, from theology to philosophical religion.

The Construction
of the History of Religion
in Schelling's Positive Philosophy

.

CONTENTS

INTRODUCTION

There is no Schelling scholarship either of the philosophical or of the theological aspects of his work, comparable in meaning and extent, for example, to Schleiermacher scholarship.[i] This is especially the case with Schelling's later philosophy. Yet Schelling is recognized as the chief representative of the development of Idealism. All of the leading idealists, including Fichte, have felt his influence. Schleiermacher and Hegel were in many ways his pupils, and through them he has had the most far-reaching influence. In the theistic philosophy of Weisse there is a direct link between him and the younger Fichte, Fechner, and others. Apparently Schopenhauer is dependent upon him; Eduard von Hartmann certainly is. Schelling's significance for particular theological schools, especially his role in providing a foundation for them in the philosophy of religion, will be noted below.

These facts alone, which are beyond dispute, should have given rise to an exhaustive Schelling scholarship. However, Schelling's philosophy in itself should provide a strong enough motive. I refer to its character as essentially a philosophy in process, a life history. An abundance of seeds are scattered in each of its periods, some developed by other thinkers, some that have remained dormant. The latter is especially the case with respect to Schelling's later periods. Historical research has therefore a twofold task: on the one hand to elaborate the permanent bases of his system, and on the other, to trace its particular lines of thought with their manifold presuppositions and complications. The first task is fundamental. But the value of Schelling scholarship for the systematic task of the present lies in the second. For in these special problems, a rich and still undeveloped material is to be found in Schelling's work.

There is a third reason for undertaking this task. As Kant's *Religion within the Limits of Reason Alone* was succeeded by the great systems of the history of religion, so today, emerging from the philosophy of religion influenced by Kant, an idealistic system of the history of religion has appeared in both the theological and philosophical camps (Troeltsch-Eucken). Under such circumstances, it may be fitting to refer anew to that form of idealist philosophy, especially philosophy of religion, which is the culmination of the whole development of Idealism, and which, with its voluntarism, realism, and positivism, stands basically nearer to modern thought than any other, notwithstanding the points where it gives great offense. Moreover, Idealism is not only a scientific movement, it is above all a religious movement. Theologians or philosophers may reject joining theology and philosophy in a unified and systematic world view. Nevertheless, they cannot avoid considering the Idealist Movement from the standpoint of the history of religion as an expression of Christian religious life. Idealism itself makes this claim, and therefore must be appreciated as such, at least in a purely historical sense. The religious self-consciousness of Idealism is characteristically expressed in Schelling's concept of "philosophical religion."

The task of the present work is to present the construction of the history of religion as the focal point of Schelling's positive philosophy. This, however, is only possible in the light of the epistemological and metaphysical principles of the whole system. Without the doctrine of the potencies one cannot even set foot in the positive philosophy. Without the concept of God and the doctrine of man, the concept of religion remains incomprehensible. The concept of history depends upon the doctrine of ideas. Because of the lack of a recognized Schelling scholarship, knowledge of these fundamentals of Schelling's system cannot be presupposed unless their meaning is made clear by the author in every case. Even then, serious difficulties appear. The "positive philosophy" belongs to that part of philosophical literature which has not only received the least scholarly attention but which is also the most problematic. Without a knowledge of the development of the concepts in Schelling's whole work, the positive philosophy remains incomprehensible. The process of their growth is in part very complicated (e.g., the doctrine of the potencies, and especially the concept of God). More thorough studies of their different aspects are needed before a full account can be given of their development.

The second part of the present work presents the construction of the history of religion. This construction is sufficiently clear in Schelling's work. The first and second parts together comprise the basis of the entire system of the "positive philosophy." The third part is devoted to the two central problems of the history of religion, the concept of religion and the concept of history. This is the focal point of the work.

Only slight use could be made of the literature on the

"positive philosophy." In general, the histories of philosophy make only brief and mostly polemical references. Kuno Fischer[ii] reports in detail, but he is too much of a reporter. He does not explain the inner relationships, especially Schelling's growth and development. Among works devoted to special problems, since most of the accounts are also mere reviews, they are not considered (Frantz, Groos, Beckers, Pfleiderer, Planck, Schaper, Dorner, etc.[iii]). Only Eduard von Hartmann offers an analysis and critique (cf. his *Schelling's Positive Philosophy as the Unity of Hegel and Schopenhauer, Schelling's Philosophical System*). But his critique is so negative, and so obviously influenced by his own standpoint, that it cannot do justice to Schelling at all (see below). Under such circumstances, the practice of quoting and refuting secondary sources is abandoned in favor of devoting more space to quotations from Schelling's work.

"Positive philosophy" signifies the subject of the entire final period of Schelling's philosophical activity. In a stricter sense, positive philosophy is to be understood in contrast to negative or rational philosophy. In each case, the context will tell whether the broader or the narrower sense is meant. The bulk of the "positive philosophy" is contained in the four volumes of the second part of Schelling's *Collected Works*. Nevertheless, volumes seven through ten of the first part come into consideration wherever there has been no fundamental progress since Schelling's philosophy of freedom.

PART I: THE EPISTEMOLOGICAL AND METAPHYSICAL STARTING POINTS OF THE HISTORICAL CONSTRUCTION

I. The General Doctrine of Principles

1. The Development of the Doctrine of the Potencies in Schelling's Philosophy

1) Ever since Kant discovered the "ground of the possibility of all knowledge, especially of experience" in the "productive synthesis of the imagination" and defined the intelligible character of the ego as freedom,[1] and ever since Fichte derived the world from the act of the absolute ego, and the young Schelling found the unconditioned in freedom, the will has been raised to an ultimate principle (1:149ff.). "To will means . . . to act absolutely." "Spirit is an original act of will" (1:395). Thus wrote Schelling in one of his earliest works. In these statements, *will* is certainly not a psychological phenomenon, but "the absolute act of freedom with which all consciousness begins" (3:576). The

43

will as phenomenon is arbitrary choice,[iv] namely, "that opposition of equally possible acts in consciousness." It is the condition "by which alone the absolute act of will can become anew an object of the ego" (3:576; 1:440).[v] Only later, when dealing with the question of the origin of the phenomenal world, was Schelling compelled to include a moment of arbitrariness in the absolute act of freedom itself. First of all, this means that "willing is the self-determination of spirit," and the act of volition in general is the supreme condition of self-consciousness, that is, it is the ultimate epistemological principle, "the act that unites theoretical and practical philosophy" (1:395). Schelling defined his relationship to Kant and his own standpoint most appropriately in this way when he said: "Therefore it is clear, that Kant's theoretical and practical philosophy are both equally groundless unless they both arise from the principle of the original autonomy of the human spirit" (1:398).

2) But whereas, for Kant, the thing-in-itself is the condition and the limit of particular knowledge, and the irrational fact of radical evil receives its possibility from the ground of intelligible freedom, and whereas, for Fichte, self-consciousness cannot be deduced unless the limit of its action is posited by the absolute ego, Schelling tries to prove from the beginning that there is an original duality in the disposition of the will. The essence of spirit is "that . . . in one and the same act, we are at the same time passive and active, determined and determining, in short, that reality (necessity) and ideality (freedom) are united in one and the same act" (1:411). Fichte's assertion, that the ego posits the nonego in absolute opposition to itself, is "theoretically considered, false," because "the original nature of spirit lies in the absolute identity of action and passion" (1:412).[2] This conception of the principle of knowledge was in fact

the ground out of which Schelling's philosophy of nature necessarily grew. It is not enough to prove that the ego is everything; rather, on the contrary, it must be understood that everything is like the ego (7:351). Nature is not an incomprehensible limit of action; it is itself action, creating will, becoming freedom, striving for consciousness. It is the gradual conquest of conscious over unconscious action until it attains equilibrium in man as a natural being. Unconscious action is real, expansive; conscious action is ideal, repulsive. Consciousness is formed from the night of the unconscious. As long as nature is the "ground of reality, or gravity," it continues to be "eternal night, an abyss of eternal silence and hiddenness in which things exist without any special life." Only "the light is the eternal affirmation of all things according to their own form of life: it is the eternal word of nature," the "cause of reality" (6:266). This formulation of Schelling's philosophy of nature expresses most clearly the fundamental notions of Schelling's cosmology and logos theory in all periods of his further development. The logos is not the ground, but the [formal] cause of reality, of things that are different and that possess form. Any estimate of Schelling's philosophical transformation must not overlook the continuity of these central points of his speculation.

3) During his Fichtean period, Schelling viewed the conflict of actions under the predominance[vi] of ideal action, and in his philosophy of nature he viewed it under the predominance of real action. With the development of his system of identity,[vii] he employed the principle of identity as his starting point to deduce both viewpoints from a higher unity. This unity can be found only beyond the conflict of actions. Hence it must not properly be described as action. Rather, identity is "action that is as still as the deepest stillness, and stillness that is as active as the highest

action" (4:305). It cannot be denied that this conception of identity, added to the connection between his own and Spinoza's system, which Schelling worked out, obscured the fundamental importance of the will, although it by no means nullified it. The unity of the affirming and the affirmed, as identity was frequently called at this time, is both self-intuition and self-affirmation, and intellectual intuition is the love with which God loves himself[3] (6:63, 556). Pure identity is now nowhere to be found in the universe; rather, only relative points of equilibrium or indifference, in which there is a quantitative predominance of either real or ideal action. Inasmuch as equilibrium is realized in man, he represents the counterpart of absolute identity, and is capable of intellectual intuition. This fundamental anthropological insight, with its implications for epistemology and philosophy of religion, has also remained Schelling's lasting possession.

Schelling calls the stages of predominance of each of the two modes of action *potencies*. The mathematical reference signifies simply the elevating or involution of one of the two factors. The task of philosophy is to construct the potencies on the basis of intellectual intuition. The fundamental epistemological character of identity makes it clear from the start that the concept of a purely real or a purely ideal action is in principle impossible. The concept of will lacking intelligibility or of intelligibility lacking will is completely foreign to Schelling.[4]

4) Soon after the conception of the system of identity, Plato's doctrine of ideas entered the horizon of Schelling's thought and was assimilated by him.[viii] Schelling's understanding of the doctrine of ideas was conditioned, 1) from a metaphysical point of view, by the synthesis of Spinoza's universalism and Leibniz's individualism, which had been achieved by Herder and Schleiermacher, and by Schelling

in his philosophy of nature, 2) from an epistemological point of view, by the Kantian and the Fichtean critique of the concept of reflection applied to the thing-in-itself and to the absolute. Thus, historically considered, there arose an unplatonic interpretation of the idea as a higher unity of abstract concept and particular thing, of unity and multiplicity. But this implies that the idea is the object of intellectual intuition: intellectual, because it contains the universal, intuition, because it contains the particular. This led further to the identification of the doctrine of ideas and the doctrine of the potencies. The most important result of this step was a further shift in approach in favor of the universal. In the philosophy of nature, nature's creative activity was directly intuited in particular natural objects. Now, by means of the concept of potencies, individual things were joined to certain comprehensive classes, so that these classes attained a greater constancy than individual things, which led to the increasing devaluation of the latter: "Therefore, in the productive process of nature, individual things are involuntarily bound to servitude and subject to futility. But those eternal forms of things are, as it were, the immediate sons and children of God" (4:223). Therefore, the world of ideas forms the middle term between the absolute and the phenomenal world. It is the object of the immediate self-affirmation of identity. "By joining limitation with infinite power, a clearer concept of the image of God arises, a conception of the necessary desire of pure affirmation mitigated by the unity of all" (7:204). Nevertheless, the problem of the phenomenal world was not solved by the interpolation of this middle term. How did it happen that the idea refused to be mitigated, and departed from the unity of all, and thence was torn asunder into individual phenomena that are transient because none of them correspond fully to their essence? The only answer is "the ancient holy doctrine . . . that souls have descended from the world of intellect to the world of sense" (6:47). But whence comes this freedom of ideas that are still the immediate children of absolute self-affirmation? They can receive it only from the absolute itself. But this implies that a principle of difference exists in indifference, a principle of self defection, an irrational principle.[5]

5) When Schelling reached this conclusion, he entered the second major period of his development, which began in 1809 with the publication of *On the Nature of Human Freedom.*[ix] The reception of this irrational moment in the absolute resulted in a powerful recurrence of the will as a principle. The original polarity in the disposition of the will, which from the standpoints of transcendental and natural philosophy could be presupposed only as given, was made problematic by a consistent exposition of the system of identity. But at the same time the ambiguous character of the will provided a solution: there is in the will itself an irrational moment, a "potency" for self-contradiction. The real, dark principle of the philosophy of nature is nothing other than the actualization of this contradiction. Freedom is the power to become disunited from oneself.[6] Consistent with the meaning of the word, Schelling now calls this power *potency*. Identity possesses the potency for freedom in the irrational. The irrational is potency κατ᾽ ἐξοχήν.[x] However, the original meaning of the concept of potency is also preserved. The potency for contradiction stands opposed to what is contradicted, as the real is in opposition to the ideal action. Nevertheless, it must never be forgotten that the question now is not with actual actions, but only with possibilities. And in this sense the name *potency* belongs especially to the first potency, whereas in the former sense the first is also the lowermost potency.

Schelling portrays the struggle of both potencies in the

world process and the gradual conquest and transfigura-
tion of the first by the second by means of the categories
of the philosophy of nature, but with the overtones of Bo-
ehmean theosophy. The irrational is the longing of the one
to give birth to itself, that is, to bring itself into existence
by conquering the darkness. But it has abandoned itself to
a chaos in which no form can be realized. Only when the
ideal is spoken as a word does chaos differentiate forms and
creatures. It [the irrational or chaos] is poverty that is wed-
ded to the idea, lawlessness that is brought to order, madness that is overcome by reason. It is the basis of every
creature, the active power of self-individuation by which
each thing attains its own; it is divine egoism that gives
power and content to divine love. The full depth of freedom is contained in man, for in him there is a perfect bond
with the ideal. Man, therefore, is free from both principles,
he is spirit. With man as spirit a new principle of far-reaching significance is attained. Even in the system of identity,
indifference to both levels of potency was found in man.
There it was merely a question of a quantitative equilibrium
that could never be regarded as a new principle. But once
the opposition of actions was conceived as resting on a
qualitative contradiction, the unification of these opposing
principles necessarily established a new principle, namely,
spirit. Spirit is to identity as actual unity is to essential unity,
as self-understanding mediated by antithesis is to immediate self-understanding. Spirit is freedom in the highest potency, raised to the highest power; it is the potency of the
goal.

Schelling postulated a triad of concepts to correspond to
this triad of potencies, and he attacked the "abstract concepts of finite and infinite" (7:371). Position is not opposed
so much to negation as to an opposite position.[7] Spirit,
which is the unity of a No and a Yes, remains spirit even

when it actualizes the No. Just this is its freedom, to be able to say No. This understanding of the concept of freedom is of far-reaching significance for the every problem. In particular, the differentiation of Schelling's two major periods rests upon it.[8] The history of the doctrine of the potencies prior to the "positive philosophy" is concluded with the elaboration of this concept. In the "positive philosophy" itself, this foundation, which was prepared beforehand, remains inviolable. Only its interpretation is new and meaningful.

2. The Exposition of the Doctrine of the Potencies in the Positive Philosophy

1) That which is [*das Seiende*] is the most original, most comprehensive, and necessary content of reason. Even though thought abstracts from every particular object, it cannot abstract from the concept of an object in general— not even when it makes itself into an object (10:233). That which is, as such, clearly lies beyond all of actual being and therefore can be called the infinite potency of being (13:-64). It is the only immediate content of thought, "with which thought moves only in itself, in its . . . ether" (13:76). In the infinite potency analytical thought discovers an inner organism of successive potencies that is "the key to all being, and the organism of reason itself. The task of rational philosophy is to reveal this organism" (13:76). Its instrument is the pure experience of thought, previously called intellectual intuition. Concerning the attempt to grasp logically the three potencies of subject, object, and spirit, it must be noted that the intellectual intuition of the concept of being is the same as the intellectual intuition of the spiritual personality in which alone being is given *in concreto* to the philosopher. This becomes clear, without a

doubt, in the voluntaristic categories that cannot be deduced logically from the concept of being, and in the line of argument, which likewise is not logically but teleologically determined: In order that there may be spirit, being must be posited as threefold. The justification of this deduction to epistemological idealism is found here, and the following exposition must be viewed from this concrete standpoint as an analysis of spirit. Finally, by joining the potencies to the concept of being, their absolute universality is emphatically displayed. This is of great significance for the interpretation of the phenomena of the history of religion.

2) The concept of *that which is* is directly opposed to actual being. It is, therefore, only infinite possibility, the potency of all being, the subject of every thing that is,[9] potential being. The concept of potentiality, which can in itself mean as many things as are logically possible, must now be thought throughout realistically (see above, ¶ 1). "Nothing except pure willing is needed in order to come into being." "Every potentiality is actually only a will that is in repose." "The will in itself is Potency κατ᾿ ἐξοχήν." "Willing is the act κατ᾿ ἐξοχήν" (13: 205). "Actual being is inconceivable apart from an act of will" (13: 206). Object means antithesis of self-assertion, and this depends only upon the will. "Even God . . . cannot conquer the will except through [the will] itself" (13: 206). The will remains potency unless it passes over into willing. But willing is in accordance with its nature. The essence of the will is to will (13: 208). But if this should happen—and it must happen immediately, unless an opposing will should prevent it—a being [*ein Seindes*] would come into existence out of its potentiality, indeed a necessary being, for there is no turning back. Just as human potentiality is power and strength that ought not to be wasted in meaningless ways (13: 208),

and just as an act cannot be taken back, and the actor is unfree with regard to it, so once potential being has become being, it has lost control of itself, it has become ecstatic (13: 209). This becomes clear in Spinozism, where it is perceived that the *potentia existendi* is whatever has come into being (12: 38). "And who is there who has not [felt] the ecstasy of Spinozism?" (13: 33) "He is startled and pushed, as it were, by being which throws a blindfold over him, he is lost in its presence,—Indeed, he is not aware of its beginning . . . therefore he has no power to oppose it, he is entirely helpless before it . . . and without even freedom" (12: 38). Freedom and history depend upon the preservation of a subjective, potential, irrational, and voluntary moment in the concept of being. So far as it concerns the potentiality of this principle, that it remain potential and not become actual being, but only the power of [actual being], it can also be called μὴ ὄν, relative nonbeing in contrast to οὐκ ὄν, absolute nonbeing (11: 288).[10] The reality of the opposition of truth and error, of good and evil, depends upon the reality of nonbeing (9: 241).[xi]

3) To preserve the potentiality of this first principle, being, in the second instance, in contrast to what can be, or potential being, must be described as actuality, as necessary being or that which is, pure and simple [*rein Seiende*]. For then it will occupy the place that potential being wants to take, so that a natural transition into being can no longer occur. Necessary being is the completely desireless and passive will. It does not have to desire to be, for it is that which is per se (13: 213). Nevertheless, it is potency, for it is a definition of that which is in general, and therefore not of an actual being, but of that which will be (13: 215). Whereas the first potency is an absolute want of being, the second is absolute fullness (12: 49). Therefore, they complement each other, and the greatest "congeniality" pre-

vails between them (12: 50). Necessary being is "the over-flowing good of essence that cannot, as it were, deny itself" (13: 51). It is the selfless in itself, whereas the first potency is the potentiality of selfishness [*das selbstisch sein Könnende*]. The latter is attracted to the former because it is poor and wants to cover its nakedness. If it were complete in itself it would draw away from the other (12: 53). All of these images only signify that the calm of absolute identity is preserved so long as the potency of subjectivity is the basis and bearer of objectivity, but that all difference will arise when subjectivity as such comes forth and wants to take the place of the objective. This conception is ultimately ethical.

Schelling's interpretation of the second potency is illus-trated by his one-sided characterization of "that vacuous absolutely impotent theism or deism, that is capable of nothing at all, which is the unique content of our so-called purely moralistic and inflated doctrine of religion" (12: 41). This doctrine lacks the "power of procreation," the power "of going forth from itself and of becoming unlike itself" (12: 41). It lacks the potency of subjectivity.

4) In the first potency, what will be is posited as pure potency. In the second potency, it is posited as pure act. Inasmuch as each excludes the other, the goal of this de-duction cannot be reached in the definition of either. Being must be posited a third time as subject-object that is free from the onesidedness of the two former principles. The freedom of the third potency is such that as subject it does not cease being object, and as object it does not cease being subject. It is that which abides by itself, which cannot lose itself, "which is actually free to be". "There is in our lan-guage no other word for this self-possessing [potency] . . . that remains potency in act, and the power to be in being, than spirit." Whereas the first potency is what can be, and the second is what must be, the third is the goal,

what ought to be or what shall be.[11] [xii] It is the potency of monotheism. But this leads from the consideration of that which is to the consideration of him who is that which is.

II. God, World, and Man

1. The Concept of God

a) The Development of the Concept of God in Schelling's Philosophy

1) The development of the doctrine of potencies is closely related to the development of the concept of God. Whereas the doctrine of potencies is an analysis of the highest principle, of identity, the concept of God receives its content from the definition of its relation to this principle. The development is completed in three stages. The first stage is distinguished by a complete identification of God and the absolute. It is from the standpoint of the philosophy of identity that Schelling begins to draw the concept of God into his system. There it can be seen from a more detailed discussion that, by equating God and identity, everything that holds true for the latter can be transferred to the concept of God.[12] To the question whether this amounts to pantheism, Schelling later answered that if pantheism means that God is equal to the sum of all things, then it must be denied, since God is rather the only true reality in contrast to things in their particularity (10: 46). But pantheism must be affirmed, if it means that God as absolute being has no freedom from his being. As absolute being, God is not the Lord of being; and being is not something that he himself posits (10: 22). By far the most important work in this period on the philosophy of religion is the *Lectures on the Method of Academic Study,* specifically the

lectures on theology and Christianity (5: 286 ff.). The significance of this work for the philosophy of history will be discussed later. The influence of Platonism on these lectures is clear, and they share with it the significance of being a transitional stage in Schelling's development. Only from the standpoint of the philosophy of freedom are all the implications of these lectures fully realized. The concept of God is construed as a trinity of the eternal, the finite, and the infinite. The eternal is God the Father, in whose yet unevolved identity the finite and the infinite are ideas "as they exist in the eternal intuition of God" (5: 294). The unqualified identification of God and the absolute is abandoned in this formulation insofar as both ideas possess independent significance. However, since true actuality is found ultimately in identity, the former identification is fundamentally not overcome.

2) This became possible only from the standpoint of the philosophy of freedom with the assertion of a real conflict within the absolute, whereby the divine self became separated from that within God which is not God himself, from the ground, from nature in God.[xiii] Schelling adapted the theosophic concept of nature in God in order to unite the immanence of things in God with their freedom. "To be separate from God, [things] must arise out of a ground different from him. But since there can be nothing outside of God, this contradiction can only be dissolved by things having their ground in that within God which is not God himself, that is, in that which is the ground of his existence" (7: 359, Gutmann). But this ground is the irrational will, the principle of subjectivity, whose contradiction of the principle of objectivity, of the will to love, is the condition of particularity, of selfhood and creaturehood. For by means of contradiction, the world process, whose task is to reconcile that which contradicts, gets underway. Every stage of

this process, whose first phase is the process of nature, presents a new form of unity of subject and object, of the irrational and the universal. In man the bond is perfect, spirit is realized, and therefore freedom for self-contradiction is once more achieved as it was in the absolute. In man, "the articulate word, the spirit is revealed, as God existing in act" (7: 364).

This leads to the second motive for positing nature in God. His nature is the ground of his existence. To exist in act, God must have an irrational ground, a nature. Not only the freedom and spirituality of the creature, but God's [freedom] as well depends on nature in God. This points directly to a view of the concept of God's aseity. The principle that God is nothing that he has not posited—this formulation of the material concept of freedom[xiv]—when considered abstractly, leads to a completely lifeless identity of the posited and the positing, which excludes every specific content—because everything definite presupposes an actual contradiction, and God is confined to the necessity of his essence, and because God becomes unfree in relation to his freedom. This substantial concept of aseity denies God the character of a spiritual personality. Only when God can really be distinguished as positing and posited can aseity become actual and living and God become spirit and personality. But this is only possible when the distinction itself is posited by God, when nature in God is his will.[13] The process of self-positing is living when it enters into contradiction. The divine self cannot posit itself in a living way unless it opposes itself, and it cannot attain perfect freedom unless it posits itself in a living way, and it cannot be a spiritual personality unless it attains perfect freedom. Just as there is a material concept of God corresponding to the material concept of freedom, so the formal concept of freedom leads to a formal rendering of the concept of God.

And whereas God was represented as the sum of actuality when the concept of substantial identity was dominant, now he is conceived as a spiritual personality. But just as the formal concept of freedom does not cancel the material concept, but actualizes it, so the concept of personality, applied to God, contributes to a vital rendering of the concept of God. And just as the concept of freedom depends upon the grasping of a new principle, so also the concept of personality is not the application of a categorial form to the trans-categorial—which would be impossible according to the critical theory of knowledge; rather, it is the intellectual intuition of spirit as the actual unity of opposing tendencies of will.

The concern, as we find it expressed in *On the Nature of Human Freedom,* to make the freedom of the creature intelligible, is the point of departure for this construction of the concept of God. The freedom of God is only a secondary consideration in this work. Even here, it is not fully elaborated. The process by which God becomes personal is the world process. The beginning, that is, the separation of God from his nature, is the beginning of the development of consciousness in God. The stages of the world process are the stages by which he becomes personal and conscious. Only in man do they reach perfection. In him God becomes self-consciousness and spirit. It is clear from this formulation that spirit and personality do not belong to God before the beginning of the world process, and, therefore, that the transition from indifference to contradiction is to be understood only as an original contingency, in von Hartmann's sense. Thus God has lost his freedom over against the world process, because he is bound to it. Further development in Schelling's philosophy begins with this deficiency in the philosophy of freedom.[14] [xiv]

3) Schelling still had the task of defining God's spiritu-

ality apart from the world process, and thereby, also, his freedom toward it. With respect to God's spirituality, it became certain ever since the development of the doctrine of freedom that "consciousness consists only in the act of becoming conscious" (8: 263). "An eternal consciousness would be unable to think, or it would be no different from a state of unconsciousness" (8: 262). It would be the condition "which we have called . . . indifference of the potencies" (7: 433). Nevertheless, if God is to attain consciousness and personality in eternity, then becoming conscious must take place eternally in him. "Now one must surely not suppose that God had been unconscious for a long time, and then became conscious. But it is possible to think that the unconscious and the conscious were included in God in the same indivisible act of becoming conscious, the conscious as the eternal present, but the unconscious as the determination of the eternal past" (8: 262). "In it [nature, the unconscious] he recognizes himself as that which was because he posits it as his eternal past. . . . In it he recognizes himself as that which is the eternal present in opposition to that which before him is an eternal past. In it he recognizes himself as what will be because he sees himself as the eternal freedom over against it, thereby seeing it as the object of a future act of will" (8: 264). The qualitative notion of time that emerges in the concept of "eternal becoming" is a foundation stone of Schelling's system, especially of his philosophy of history. It will be examined more closely in that connection. In any case, at this point it frees the concept of God from a way of thinking that joins it indissoluably to the world process. The text just quoted shows this clearly: nature, posited as the past, is the possible object of a future act of will. But this means that it is potency, or rather the system of three potencies, for potency, in the meaning of the word that now emerges, is exactly the power to posit being outside of God (see above). In nature, which becomes potency in the eternal process, in his nature, which is potentiated threefold, God has the possibility to will a world process, but now in freedom. God is spirit and personality not only through the actual world process, but rather through the potencies of every future process. These ideas have been brought to perfect clarity in the presentation of the concept of God in the positive philosophy.[15]

b) The Concept of God in the Positive Philosophy

1) The account of the doctrine of the potencies has anticipated one aspect of the concept of God. Therefore we begin with the other aspect in order to consider next the relation of each aspect to the other and [finally] the entire construction. Schelling begins with Kant's doctrine of the ideal of pure reason. "We cannot resist the thought any more than we can endure it, that a being, which we represent as the highest among all possible beings, should, as it were, say to itself: I am from eternity to eternity, beyond me there is nothing except what is willed by me. But whence am I? Here everything sinks beneath us" (13: 163).[xvi] Kant's statement leads to the concept of being that is prior to all thought, to "primordial being," the necessity of being that is prior to all thought, that is the veritable abyss of human reason. It is the actuality that precedes all possibility, the beginning of all thought, and, therefore, is itself unthinkable. In the face of this being reason can do nothing; it is devoured by it. It is that whose existence is undoubted. The being of everything that proceeds from potency is doubtful, for potency is potential being and potential nonbeing. Therefore, doubt is excluded by that which precedes all potency (13: 242). Philosophical doubt arises in connection with a particular existing thing. It asks

whether it is truly that which is. Hence doubt always presupposes true being. But thought cannot prove that there
is such a being, for the ultimate question always remains:
why is there anything at all? Why is there not nothing?
There is no answer here except the immediate certainty
that something exists. If primordial being is prior to every
concept, then even the concept of God cannot be applied
to it. For then it would be something, it would have a
concept. But it is a priori inconceivable. It is the *prius* of
divinity, that which can be God (13: 160). If God were only
this *prius*, then he would be the absolute in the sense of the
absolutely unrelated.

2) But God is God because of his relationship to the
potencies. "If God has his *prius* in act, then he will have his
divinity in the potencies, thus he is *potentia universalis*, [and]
as that which transcends being he is the Lord of Being" (13:
160). His "Lordship" (10: 262) consists in his ability to be
that which is, to help it to be. That which is, "the idea of
possibility as a whole," has no existence, for "the universal
as such does not exist, only the particular. The universal
essence exists only if it is the absolute individual" (11: 586).
If God were only being itself [*das Sein selbst*], then he would
be bound to being, unfree before it, and unhappy, as is
everything that bears the shackles of being (10: 265). "But
God is God because he is free to be and not to be; there
is no other concept of God." Newton said it correctly, "God
is *vox relativa.*" "*Deitas est Dominatio Dei*" (10: 261).[xvii]. His
realm is being, and corresponds in a threefold sense to the
triad of potencies: in the sense of the first potency it is the
power to set the potencies in tension and thereby to come
into existence; in the sense of the second potency it is the
power within the world process to return the first potency
to potentiality; in the sense of the third potency [it is
power] to remain Lord also "of beings who are brought

back from estrangement" (10: 271). By means of his relationship to being, "the a priori inconceivable in God
[becomes] conceivable" (13: 165). That being which precedes all thought, the *prius* of divinity, proves to be God by
its lordship over being, and at the same time it gives itself
in relation to the concept in that it is that which is and
causes it to be.

Schelling now applies the concept of identity to the relation of the divine *prius* and the potencies. "God contains in
himself nothing but the pure *that* of his own being. But
there would be no truth in saying that he exists if he were
not something—something indeed not in the sense of a
thing that is but of everything that is—and if he were not
related to thought, not to a single concept but to the concept of concepts, to the idea. Here is the true locus for that
unity of being and thought" (10: 587). "But in this unity,
priority is not on the side of thought; being is the first" (11:
587). The universal, the idea, does not have the power to
realize itself. Rather, the individual, indeed, the absolute
individual—in whom there is no *what*, only *that*—realizes
itself, makes itself intelligible and enters the circle of reason and knowledge, "by becoming itself the universal, all-
comprehending essence, by clothing itself with essence"
(11: 588).

3) This construction is summed up in the assertion
that God is perfect spirit. He is spirit, inasmuch as he includes within himself the triad of his mode of being, and he
is perfect spirit because he is free from each one of these
three forms. He is not even bound to the third. "The absolute spirit is the ever-free spirit, free even from himself and
from his being as spirit." "This state of being bound not
even to oneself gives him, at first, that absolute, transcendent, overwhelming freedom, the thought of which so
. . . extends all the vessels of our thought and knowledge,

that we feel . . . that we have reached that than which
nothing higher can be thought. Freedom is our highest
[thought], our divinity, which we choose as the ultimate
cause of all things" (13: 256). God is free from each of his
forms, because in each of them he is the whole spirit, because his unity is indivisible; because he remains the All-
One [*das All-Einige*] even in the separation of his potencies
(13: 269). Schelling defines monotheism as the doctrine
that God as perfect spirit is the All-One. The traditional
doctrine of the uniqueness of God, "that there is no other
God beside God" (13: 13), is an empty tautology that in fact
defines mere theism, the dogma of God in general. But the
proposition [that God is perfect spirit] asserts that outside
God there is nothing at all; that he is the absolutely only
one. Not the existence of another God, but every other
existence is denied. "If theology understands the doctrine
of the only God only from the position of so-called negative
attributes, that is, God precedes and is outside every . . .
relation, if, in this way, it limits the meaning of monotheism
to this negative unity" (12: 61n), then it lacks a proper
concept of monotheism. But "only he can be called the only
God who is the All-One according to his concept, who is
not unique in a negative, exclusive sense" (12: 61). He is
the All-One because by him alone being is, "because the
modalities of the divine being must be the modalities of the
whole of being" (12: 60). But he is the One, because in
none of his forms is he God for himself, "but only as their
bond and indissoluable (spiritual, personal) unity" (12:
61).

   Schelling now contrasts this concept of monotheism with
theism and pantheism. "Theism is that concept in which
God in general is posited"[16] (12: 70). It is a mere privation
inasmuch as it does not lead to the knowledge of the only
God. It is indefinite and requires something more to define

it. It is therefore even incapable of distinguishing itself from pantheism, for although it affirms the personality of God, it clearly cannot grasp it (Jacobi). To be sure, theism asserts a [divine] self-consciousness, "but a self-consciousness is inconceivable without positing in self-consciousness at least three intrinsic distinctions" (12: 73). Although it affirms a free creation, its God is absolutely impotent and is not able to depart from himself. That fundamental concept "according to which God is the immediate potency of being, and therefore the potency of all of being, and, in return, according to which all of being is only the being of God, this fundamental concept is the nerve of all religious consciousness which is moved in its depths by the mere mention of it" (12: 69). Both the understanding and feeling are dissatisfied with this "vacuous theism" because it lacks this principle. On the other hand, the spell of pantheism lies in its emphasis on this principle, and it can be overcome only by giving this principle its due, as ground or basis. Taken absolutely and for itself, the immediate power of being amounts to the blind, unmoved being of Spinoza's substance, which is unknown to itself. But when it is conceived as potency (see above), then the true concept of God is attained. "Monotheism is nothing else than pantheism that has become esoteric, concealed and inward; it is pantheism that has been overcome" (12: 69).

The concept of monotheism necessarily leads to a doctrine of unity [*All-Einheitslehre*] concretely conceived, corresponding to the threefold potency of being, to the doctrine of tri-unity [*Drei-Einheitslehre*]. Monotheism and trinity are basically identical. Monotheism has become world-historical only as the doctrine of the trinity (12: 76). Nevertheless, they cannot be simply equated. Although the Christian doctrine of the trinity has the same content as monotheism, its content is raised to the highest level (12:79). But this

elevation takes place historically, and can only be understood according to the principles of "historical philosophy" at the point in the development [of history] where it
is realized.[17]

c) *The Concept of God as the Highest Principle of Knowledge:*
Negative and Positive Philosophy
1) In the divine self there is no "what," it is pure
"that," and in the infinite potency of being there is no
"that," it is pure "what." Nevertheless, they stand together
in the highest unity, "so that whatever always is must be
related to a concept; whatever is nothing at all, i.e., whatever has no relation to thought, is also not true" (11: 587).
Thus everything can be considered in two ways. Reason
concerns itself with knowledge of the in-itself, of the concept, of the essence of things. It deduces a priori the content, the material of that which is, and in this connection it
is entirely incidental to the concept whether something
actually exists. Indeed, if anything exists, it must exist just
as thought necessarily conceives it. In grasping the real,
reason does not comprehend reality (13: 61). The infinite
potency of being, that which is, potentiated threefold [*das
dreifach potenzierte Seiende*], together with the plenitude of all
possible combinations of the potencies, corresponds to
reason construed as the infinite potency of knowledge. But
it is still potency. The entire rational or negative philosophy moves about in [the realm of] potency. Negative
philosophy can never attain to the status of act or of actual
existence. It would never even occur to it to choose to
prove that an object of experience exists. It would be as
superfluous as it is unnecessary (13: 58). In Kant's critique
of the divine proofs it is clearly stated that it is impossible
to deduce existence from a concept. Fichte has clearly conceived the idea of a science of reason that is separated from
everything factual (13: 55 ff.). Hegel tried to construct a

pure system of the science of reason, but he failed because he claimed much more, specifically in the transition from logic to the philosophy of nature, by using categories like "release" [*Entlassen*] and "fall" [*Abfall*], and later on he fell back on the concept of creation, thereby trespassing upon the positive philosophy[18] [xviii](13: 87 ff.).

2) Whereas God as infinite potency is the starting point of rational philosophy, God as absolutely transcendent being is the principle of positive philosophy. Whereas rational philosophy is aprioristic and deductive, positive philosophy is aposterioristic and empirical. Experience is the only means of proof in positive philosophy. It does not belong to positive philosophy to prove the *prius* of divinity itself; "it is beyond all proof, it is the absolute beginning known only by itself" (13: 129); it is not only prior to every thought, but also to every being that is present in experience—the latter is always related to thought. It is the "that" which excludes all multiplicity in itself, and which rules in all things (11: 590). Positive philosophy is supposed to prove the divinity of this *prius,* that is, to verify that [God as *prius*] has entered into a relationship with that which is and has shown himself as the Lord of being. God can be proved only if he proves himself, and whether he proves himself depends upon his will. "Only decision and act can establish a genuine experience" (13: 114). But because "the realm of actuality is incomplete . . . the proof is also never complete" (13: 131). In this sense, positive philosophy is not a system, but a philo-sophia (13: 132). Its concrete tasks are to consider the creation as the freely posited beginning of the world process; the Fall as the beginning of the evolution of the history of religion; and the evolution of the history of religion, which culminates in revelation. The last, which is the absolute proof of the divinity of God, is also the primary subject matter of positive philosophy.

2. The Beginning of the World Process: The Creation of the World of Ideas

1) The divinity of God, his lordship over his being, consists concretely in his freedom to posit being external to the divine. The possibility for this derives directly from the ambiguous character of the first potency. This possibility appears to the perfect spirit as something unforeseen. To be sure, [it appears] from eternity, but not on account of his will, for it lies hidden in his nature. [It appears] neither according to his will, nor against it, rather it is gladly perceived, for "the appearance of the first possibility of a being different from himself frees him for the first time from the necessity of his primordial being . . . this appearance gives him to himself for the first time by freeing him from that holy and indeed supernatural but inviolable Necessity *(Ananke)* whose arms, as it were, first received him" (13, 268). Now he becomes aware of his absolute freedom. He does not need to maintain unity with being, because being is his essence. In conformity with [his] being he can posit the separation of the potencies and thereby a being "that is different from his eternal being or essence" (13: 269). For "I will be what I will be" (13: 270). The Lordship of God over the separated potencies is founded in the second potency which, inasmuch as it is the middle [potency], furnishes the mediating possibility of creation through the first potency. As soon as potential being is raised to being, infinite subjectivity passes from potency into act, and the second potency, that which is as such, or infinite objectivity, becomes potential. But as a consequence the living unity of the [third] potency, of spirit, is destroyed, and, by virtue of the unity inherent in the divine life, there begins a process of the gradual conquest of the first potency and [its] return to potentiality. Every step is likewise a recovery and realiza-

tion of the third potency, of what ought to be. This is the beginning of the concrete, for, in its pure burning that is not yet assuaged, the infinite subjectivity of all creation is a hostile consuming fire (13: 289). Only if it is covered over and hidden does it become the basis of every creature (13: 290). Creation from nothing is creation from that which is not, that is, from potential being (10: 285), from μὴ ὄν not from οὐκ ὄν.

2) Inasmuch as creation is due to an adaptation or "dissimulation" of the potencies, it is deemed divine dissimulation or irony. God acts deceptively by displaying the opposite of what he wants, by appearing to affirm what he intends to negate (12: 91f.). "It is not given to everyone to understand the deep irony of all divine activity. Whoever . . . has not already grasped it in the [divine] governance of the world will not understand it at all . . . later, specifically, in connection with the doctrine of redemption" (14: 24). One must ask genial rationalists whether they have ever noticed that God is a genius who has little regard for what they call rational (Hamann) (14: 24). This idea is at the very heart of the romantic doctrine of irony, which originally was an aesthetic concept, but gradually came to have a religious use. "It is the highest task of art to represent an infinite content . . . in the most perfect, that is, the ultimate form—a content that intrinsically resists form and appears to destroy every form"[19] (14: 25). God, the great ironist, performs this task in the creation and in the world-[historical] process: in the creation until the most perfect [is reached] in man, for "the way of creation does not proceed from narrow to broad, but from broad to narrow" (11: 494); and in the world-[historical] process by means of the divine folly, the absolute paradox of the cross of Christ (14: 24). The divinity of God exists precisely in the power of this contradiction, "of this absurdity, if you will, of being

the one who at the same time affirms and denies, who nevertheless does not depart from but remains what he is" (14: 25). The religious consciousness of Idealism is centered in this protest against "the law of contradiction as it has been commonly understood" (14: 25). Thus it stands with Christianity in a common struggle against natural reason. The negative in the dialectical method is the negation of natural cognition.[20] In the doctrine of the "dissimulation" of the potencies there is a twofold evaluation of creation: it both reveals God and conceals him. This doctrine becomes the basis of the interpretation of paganism and unbelief, for, according to Schelling, these, and not monotheism and faith, are in need of interpretation (see below).

3) As long as Schelling conceived the world process as the personalizing of God, the question of a motive for creation had no meaning. An original contingency was its beginning, and necessity its progress. But the concept of motive comprises a synthesis of freedom and necessity, which in principle should only be conceived ethically, but which resists conceptual understanding. Therefore, in the account [of creation] each side [freedom and necessity] must be presented separately, and the conception of the unity of the intellectual intuition of the ethical mode must be abandoned. Schelling's exposition of the motive for the creation of the world must be considered according to this presupposition.

With reference to the moment of freedom, Schelling makes clear that the proper motive for creation can only be the creature, since it could not come into being apart from the process of creation (13: 277). The same idea is expressed more precisely in another way: God extricates being from the unconscious blessedness of the substantial unity of the potencies and delivers it over to becoming and suffering, so that it may live with him in conscious and self-posited unity and blessedness. For an unconscious blessedness is to be regarded as no [blessedness], and "whatever is not God either has no part at all in divine joy, or can attain joy only through sorrow, and glory only through suffering"[21] (10: 266). This statement expresses with complete clarity that no necessity of any kind exists for God. Nevertheless, in return, he is related to being, it is *his* being, and this leads to the moment of necessity in the creation. In a theosophical idiom that even he considered bold, Schelling describes this aspect [of creation]: In his three potencies God possesses beginning, middle, and end within each other. Because of this indissolubility, God's attempt to comprehend himself in his different forms would immediately drive him from one form into another. The result would be a futile and unhappy circular movement. Only when God actually separates beginning and end does he possess himself in the different forms of his essence (13: 273). When the theosophical overtones are removed from this thought, what is left is the already frequently mentioned [idea] of conscious self-positing that takes place by the conquest of a negation. Now, however, this self-positing is not to be conceived as the means by which God becomes self-conscious, but as the conscious realization of love within God, that is, in a trinitarian way.[22] For the sake of the free community of love within himself, God created the world out of love for the creature.

4) One can speak of a freely posited community of love within God only if the relative autonomy of the divine potencies is presupposed. But this is conceivable only if God endows each of the three potencies with a separate will, if he is other than that which actualizes the will of the first potency, and other than that which puts the second potency in opposition to the first, and, finally, other than that which

makes for the unity of both. Only where there is an autonomous will is there personality. To be sure, prior to the tension of the potencies there is an eternal unity, but no tri-unity, for there is no place here for a separate will. A separate object is lacking. The eternal word remains unspoken because God still has the will of the ground, which must be persuaded and formed and restrained. Only when the first potency rises into being is the second compelled once more to posit itself in opposition to it. Schelling describes this process as the generation of the Son. "Now the act in which any being posits another being uniform but external to itself . . . a being that does not come forth full-blown, but is so posited that it must realize itself in a necessary and unceasing act . . . must be called generation" (13: 312). Generation is completed with the completion of the natural process.[23] Now the Son has a will of his own. But his will is really the will of the father, who is concealed behind the mask of the potencies. "The essence of the Son is to be the will that seeks not its own. The Son, as it were, has no will of his own, rather his will is really . . . the true will of the Father, who cannot reveal it directly, and who therefore invests it . . . in the Son" (13: 325). The will of the spirit is realized only when the generation of the Son is completed. He cannot come before the Son is glorified.

With the generation of the Son, the development of science [*Wissenschaft*] has reached a point where monotheism must be affirmed not merely as a concept, but as a dogma, that is, as a principle that bears in itself a conscious negation, namely, the [negation] of multiplicity in God. Only after the separation of the potencies is unity *as* unity posited[24] (13: 281).

3. The End of the Natural Process and the Beginning of History

a. Man as the Central Idea

1) The first potency has been led outside itself, outside its potentiality. The goal of the natural process is to restore it to itself. In this way, "coming-to-itself, self-consciousness" arises. "The entire [natural] process is merely a coming-to-itself of that which is self-consciousness in man" (13: 287). The natural process is emerging consciousness, which begets man. With his birth, nature as such is completed, and the potentiality of its organization is exhausted (10: 112). For in man the three potencies are united: Man is God realized in the creature. "Because divinity finds its goal and repose only in man, therefore it has endowed him with so much" (10: 272). God is to be revealed as God only within man, and not in the tension of the potencies in the natural process (10: 273). Through the separation of the cosmic powers, his light is diffused everywhere, but in man it is beamed within *radio directo* and is directly related to him (13: 344). Schelling's anthropology is summed up in this statement: "The pure substance of human consciousness . . . is such that in itself and by its very nature it posits God" (12: 119). There are three points to be considered in this proposition: I. Only human consciousness is under discussion here, because "the original man is . . . in essence pure consciousness" (12: 118). Indeed, he is the one who has fully come to himself. Anything not transfigured into consciousness would deprive him of this character. II. Pure substance is, in itself, *natura sua,* consciousness that is God positing. Here we have to do not with a contingent relation to God mediated by a negation, but with an immediate, original, and substantial relation. III. Man posits God, not merely by reflecting God's image, but by realizing the tri-unity of the potencies concretely,

and by restoring them after their separation in the natural process.

2) As the unity of the three potencies, man is spirit and, therefore, freedom. For "the principle of being that is external to God can exist only in an act that is like God" (11: 431). Man is not God, but godlike, therefore he can also be called the anti-divine. He has the potentiality to set himself in opposition to God (11: 461, *sic.*). "The full force of the dark principle is in man as well as the whole power of light. In him is the deepest abyss and the highest heaven" (7: 363). Because he is the perfect unity of both principles, he is spirit, that is, he is free from both.[25] He can actualize once again the potency of the ground that has become his basis. This is his freedom. But because the unity of the principles (light and dark) is not indissoluable in him, as it is in God, and because he is not above the potencies but is their product, his freedom is therefore a freedom for good and evil.

3) The original natural process has reached its goal. It is posited by God and conforms to his norm. Its result is the world of ideas, namely, that system of the indifference of the first and second potencies, of subject and object, [which is constituted] in the third potency, spirit. Man stands at the point of absolute indifference. He embraces both orders [the natural and the ideal]. He is their point of unity, their central idea, the idea κατ᾽ ἐξοχὴν He mediates between the universal idea that stands under the exponent of the real, that is, nature, and the idea in ideal potency [*die ideel potenzierte Idee*], the spirit world[26] (14: 292). Because nature has its point of unity in him, man has power over it. The errors of magic and alchemy indicate a recollection of this power, which is restored in the miracles of revelation (13: 362). And "just as the multitude of things in nature strive after unity and are themselves complete

and, as it were, happy only in this unity, so it is with the multitude in the human world" (7: 460). But its unity is God (7: 461). Of this world of the idea, "the immanence of things in God is to be absolutely affirmed" (13: 353). The world of ideas is external to God only in the sense of *praeter,* not of *extra deum* (13: 352).[xix]

b. The Fall of the World of Ideas as the Suprahistorical Presupposition of History

1) "The creation was complete, but it was placed on a movable foundation" (13: 359). It was founded on man's freedom. "God valued the freedom and spontaneity of the creature so highly that he subjected the fate of his entire creation to the free will of the creature" (13: 359). God did not desire the involuntary and untried blessedness of the creature (12: 144). The cosmic law of nemesis does not permit indecision after the potency of all ambiguity has emerged from its hiddenness. Only when all darkness has been transfigured into light can the process come to an end. As far as it can be said, "God himself, as it were, presses irresistibly upon the world" (13: 359), "[the Fall] must occur, as it were, by virtue of a purely natural will," "therefore, the more everything is circumscribed, the more intelligibility will arise" (13: 360). Nevertheless, the Fall does not occur because of any strict necessity, and it cannot be proved a priori (13: 360). The problem of motivation here is analogous in every way to the problem of motivation as it relates to creation and redemption.

2) Man's freedom is such that he can do what God did when he began his work of creation; he can set the potencies in tension. And just as the possibility of another being appears to the creator in the ambiguous nature of the first potency, so there arises in the creature, by means of the same potency, the temptation to be like God. Finally, just

as the creation is the creator's disguise, so temptation bears the mark of deceit (12: 151). For it is an error for man to believe that he can remain lord of the potencies even when he has set them in tension. As soon as it is kindled and raised to a higher power, the principle of subjectivity, which in the potential state is the basis of every creature, attempts to negate every creature. As long as man chooses to be the universal essence, he remains in the center, and is the lord of the potencies. But when, as an individual being, he wants to become lord of the potencies, he becomes subject to that which ought not to be [*das Nichtsein-Sollende*] that is, he becomes subject to that which ought to remain potential [*Potenz-bleiben-Sollende*]. Sin is not something negative, but it is also not absolutely positive. Rather, it is that which is not but which desires to be. Hence it is a lie (7: 366).

3) The Fall has occurred. The entire condition of the world testifies to it, for the Fall of the central idea [i.e., man] has cosmic significance. After consciousness was dismembered—that first consciousness in which everything was to have unity and stability—the external, dismembered world arose, lacking inwardness. There arose also false, merely phenomenal time which, cut off from its true future, always·repeats itself in an unhappy and monotonous uniformity (13: 352). In this sense Fichte is right: Man posits the world, namely, this world that is enslaved by the power of subjectivity, and has fallen into the antithesis of particularity and abstraction, fallen away from the idea. This fallen world is under the rule of transitoriness, for which space, time, and categories are only different expressions. "The whole earth is a great ruin" (9: 33). Also the unity of ideal man has been dismembered by the Fall. He chose to be a particular being; now he has become subject to the principle of separation. By becoming an individual, he gave

unlimited possibility to equally individual wills, of which each one is only a realization of the supra-temporal self-positing act. And this "unfathomable act of selfhood of a single individual is also the act by which this world—the world outside the idea—is posited for everyone" (11: 464). With individuation comes the necessity of death. No individual attains the idea of manhood, therefore whatever is not ideal man in him must be cast away by death. "The necessity of death presupposes two absolutely irreconcilable principles, whose separation is death" (7: 474). These principles may not be equated with body and soul (the founder of the philosophy of nature had rejected from the start the idea of an immortal soul without a basis in nature) but rather with that which truly is and that which is not but which wants to be[27] (7: 475).

It can now in fact be asserted that the world posited by the Fall is outside God in the sense of *extra deum*. Schelling expresses this also by saying that the world of ideas becomes ideal on account of the Fall. It has no reality, just as the world of appearances has no ideality. It exists only in consciousness. But since the Fall the principle of unconsciousness is predominant. Ideality and reality are separated from one another. Divine indifference is destroyed. God is no longer united to his will in the world.

4) God is no longer united to his will in the world. But he is there as displeasure and wrath. "God still effects this world, but not, as originally, its essence. . . . As long as the world is external to him, he only effects its substance, not its form" (13: 372). After man has raised it anew, the will of the ground becomes an enemy to creatures and a destroyer. It becomes the principle of divine wrath.[28] It is the right of actualized subjectivity to destroy the creature. "This is the profound scriptural doctrine of divine wrath, which a superficial exegesis has attempted to erase in vain"

(13: 373) This doctrine can also be expressed in trinitarian terms: God is no longer related to the world as Father, for only by the generation of the Son in the world process is he Father. But on account of the Fall, the Son, that is, the will of the second potency, has lost his lordship over being. Word and light have been devoured by disorder and darkness, and as it is with the Word, so is it also with the Spirit. It is the same as it was in the beginning of the natural process. The first potency is in act, the second and the third are in potentiality. To be sure, the potencies continue to have the same significance that they had within God: they cannot cease being personality in itself, and they retain the consciousness of their divinity (13: 368). But a new process is necessary to restore their lordship over being. This process is history.

PART II: THE HISTORY OF RELIGION[1]

A. MYTHOLOGY

I. The Starting Point: Absolute Prehistoric Time and the Transition to History

1) History is essentially history of religion. This assumption follows directly from Schelling's anthropology. Human consciousness is substantially God-realizing consciousness. Immediacy is lost on account of the Fall. Through the mediation of history, a conscious realization of God will take place. History is the process in which consciousness becomes indirectly what it was directly, namely, religious in the absolute sense. Everywhere, the cultural process has its roots in the religious, and in its completion it returns to it. Even the cultural process can be viewed from the standpoint of the history of religion.

The presupposition of all history is the suprahistorical fact of the fall of the world of ideas (11: 184). However, the immediate result of the Fall, is not actual history, but rather the possibility of history, that is, a prehistorical condition. Prehistorical, not in the sense of something that comes before history, but rather factually, as a situation in which nothing happens that transcends the natural functions. We must think of this condition as a kind of eternity that only becomes time, that is, time past, by means of historical time. The strict separation of historical time from prehistorical time is of great significance for the philosophy of history. Because of this separation, there is no longer a limitless history lost in the past, but rather times that are actually, that is, qualitatively, different from each other. "The primal moment, namely, the beginning," is no longer lacking (11: 232). It is necessary to assume a prehistorical condition because every history, at the very least, presupposes a duality of principles that contend with each other. However, on account of the Fall, consciousness has come under the control of the first potency, which seized it and, what is more, keeps it for the present in a condition analogous to that total unconsciousness which prevailed before the beginning of the natural process. The nature of the actualized ground, which is hostile to everything concrete, conscious, and spiritual, becomes manifest here. Mankind lives in a calm, still undisturbed unity. Its unity is God, as it was for ideal man. An original, but relative monotheism can be ascribed to mankind, for the possibility of another God had not yet appeared to consciousness, although in fact it was there. This monotheism lacked comprehensiveness; it was monotheism mythologically conceived. It was "in fact a genuine polytheism, because it had not abolished the possibility of other gods" (11: 127). "Polytheism was ordained for mankind, not in order to destroy the true One, but the one-sided One, that is, in order to destroy a merely relative monotheism" (11: 139).

2) Prehistoric time came to an end as soon as the second

potency began to have an effect upon consciousness in order to break the predominance of the first. Then came the time of transition, which was fulfilled "by that tremendous vibration of human feeling and knowledge that produced the images of the folk-gods" (13: 380)—folk-gods, because corresponding to the religious confusion that was just beginning, there was a dissolution of the unity of mankind into nations, tribes, and races. Nothing can separate a race or a nation from another except mythology, which defines the inmost essence of the spirit (11: 94). Even language, the direct expression of spirit, depends upon mythology. This is typically portrayed in the story of the Tower of Babel, which manifests a genuine recollection of that moment when the second potency appeared from afar to consciousness, and mankind was seized by a fear of the loss of unity[2] (11: 105). Paganism, like folk-culture, is a confusion of tongues (11: 105). The transition to history was now complete, so that every race broke away from the common humanity and identified itself with that stage of the mythological process whose representative it was destined to become (13: 380). However, the mythological process is not confined to the primary bearers of its development. With every advance there is a common vibration in the entire consciousness of mankind, whose traces can be found everywhere among races that either represent a higher stage of the mythological process or among those who do not participate in the principal development of history. This development itself is conditioned by the successive advances of the potencies that were united in original consciousness and are being progressively reunited (13: 395, sic.). Moreover, there is an incessant struggle of the second, forward-driving potency against the first that resists it, a struggle that will not end until the third potency is fully realized. Inasmuch as the potencies have trinitarian significance, this process, occurring in human consciousness, is theogonic, as was the natural process, and it is analogous to it in its outcome. "The primary task of the philosophy of mythology is . . . to identify in the successive mythologies of the races the different moments in the theogonic process, that process which generates mythology" (13: 381).

II. The Mythological Process

1. The First Epoch: Relative Prehistoric Time and the Transition to History—Uranos

In its first assault, the second potency is unable to overcome the predominance of the first. The latter holds its ground. However, in the rotation that maintains the equilibrium of powers it is broken up into particular centers analogous to the division of the basis of the natural process into the heavenly bodies. The result is astral religion, which, according to Greek nomenclature, may be designated Uranos worship. However, just as the stars are "not inorganic or organic entities, or stones, or plants, or beasts," so what comes to be worshiped in them is also "not nature, but what abides before and beyond nature" (12: 175). It is impossible to suppose that the stars were first thought to be something else, and then were made into gods: "as if man could turn whatever he wanted into God" (12: 184). He was, as it were, carried off by nature, and became beside himself and ecstatic on account of the predominance of that principle. "But it is entirely absurd to suppose the contrary, to think that he has the same free and rational relationship to nature that we have ourselves; as if the stars could be perceived by him as mere natural objects, and afterwards be endowed with divinity" (12:

184f.). Astral religion is the system of Zabism.[xx] It appeared in an age that is still relatively prehistorical, when the strange god was rejected. The cultural condition that corresponds to it is nomadic. To later consciousness, Uranos is the god of the golden age when consciousness was undivided, uninhibited, and absolutely dependent (12: 183). Therefore its decline was the first grief, to which lamentations everywhere testify: "There is a lamentation for the lost god throughout the whole of mythology. Longing follows him and calls him back" (12: 273).

2. The Second Epoch: Persia, Babylonia, and Arabia—Urania

The second potency attempts to restore the first to a condition of potentiality, to make it the basis, the matter of its [the second potency's] own realization. When something becomes matter for another higher reality, it becomes, for mythological consciousness, its mother. Every genuine change in mythology occurs when the god changes into a woman, when he becomes the mother of the god who is to come (12: 193). Thus Uranos becomes Urania. Urania marks the effective beginning of the mythological process. She is revered by the oldest races: as Mitra by the Persians, although on account of the reaction led by Zoroaster her cultus was soon suppressed; as Mylitta by the Babylonians; and as Astarte by the inhabitants of Felix-Arabia. But whereas the coming of the new god among the Persians was prevented by Zoroaster's reaction, and whereas among the Babylonians the strange god was always experienced as a stranger, and as one still to come, among the Arabians the son of the goddess was well known. But conversion to the strange god was made to appear as a sacrilege by the power that had dominated consciousness until then. Hence the inability to interpret various religious acts symbolically, that is, the inability to reflect upon them freely. Instead, these acts were believed to be inspired, that is, necessitated by the inner condition of consciousness (13: 248f.). This explains the solemn, public act of adultery committed by every Babylonian woman in the temple of Mylitta with a stranger—the strange god, for Uranos's becoming a woman is represented as castration and "consciousness has become so united with the god in this whole process, and so intimately bound up with him, that whatever happens to it is experienced as if it had happened to the god, and *vice versa*" (12: 249). This also accounts for temple prostitutes, castration, bisexual gods, men dressed as women and the reverse (cf. the Old Testament prohibitions) (12: 251).

3. The Third Epoch

a. The First Period: Canaanites and Phoenicians—Kronos

As long as the second god was represented only as the one to come, or as a child, the first god was indulgent. But when the new potency appeared in force, the old was aroused by it. The old god appeared once more as a masculine god; the one whom the Greeks call Kronos. Kronos is Uranos. But, inasmuch as he now has an opposing principle, he is a concrete god, the god of a specific age (12: 287). Here in connection with the individualizing of divinity in Kronos, an attempt was made for the first time to represent the god through images. These representations intentionally (not because of inability) avoid attributing humanlike, spiritual traits to Kronos's character (12: 293), for the age of Kronos corresponds to inorganic nature, a crude and shapeless mass, in which, at the very best, spirit is deadened by all natural objects (12: 293). His people are the Canaanites, the Phoenicians, and the Carthaginians, who worship him as Baal and Moloch. Kronos can "exclude the liberating god, whom an earlier consciousness had borne, from divinity, but no longer from being. . . . Hence the latter must give up his right to divinity and assume the form of a servant" (12: 307). One such demigod is Melkarth of the Phoenicians (the bringer of royal culture). In order that Melkarth might remain with them, and in order that he might not be excluded from being by Kronos—in which case, Kronos would become Uranos once more (for he is Kronos only by virtue of the opposing principle)—firstborn sons were sacrificed to Kronos by the Phoenicians (12: 322). Consciousness experiences the approaching freedom from the first god as a blood-demanding guilt (12: 300). The sacrifices are sin-offerings caused by consciousness's fear of losing god. "On account of consciousness's deepest error, the awakening of freedom appears as a sacrilege" (12: 274). The sin-offerings brought to Moloch are the most telling witnessess of the reality of the power that creates mythology. The Greek Heracles corresponds to Melkarth. Because of divine jealousy and a strange guilt, this demigod suffered and served, having been reduced to the form of a servant. All the blessings of a truly worthy human existence were ascribed to him. In the end he sacrificed his human part and was exalted to pure divinity (12: 331).

b. The Second Period: Phrygians and Thracians—Cybele

A new materialization followed the reaction of the first potency in Kronos. It led to the effective conquest of the first god. Kronos became Cybele, the goddess of the Phrygo-Thracian race. With her, polytheism became fully explicit. She is the great mother of the gods. Her manifestation is accompanied by the orgy, the frenzy of consciousness that has suddenly become free (12: 351).

Kronos's (Attis's) transformation is always represented here as castration. Castrated priests follow her; the phallus is her sign of victory (12: 352). Hypnotic music that causes madness makes consciousness blind to the loss of its original unity and the advent of a multitude of gods (12: 362). The natural event corresponding to Cybele's appearance is the organization of matter (12: 356). She is the one who descends from the mountains, and like the fruitful earth spreads herself on the hills and the plains (12: 354). Therefore she is worshiped as the benefactress of agriculture and civilization.

  c. *The Third Period*

i. Egypt—Typhon, Osiris, Horos

Egyptian mythology is nothing else "than the death-throe of the real principle in its final convulsion" (12, 356). Typhon is the embodiment of the real principle, Osiris, of the ideal. In the beginning, consciousness is in such a state of uncertainty that it sometimes lets Typhon be defeated, and sometimes Osiris. The uncertainty of the mythological consciousness is observed in a mythological form, in Isis, who at an earlier time was believed to be the wife of Typhon, and who commits adultery with Osiris. Later, as the wife of Osiris, she sets the imprisoned Typhon free. Only the instability and vacillation of consciousness can explain the profusion of adultery and incest among the holiest of divinities. "It must never be supposed that an entire race or any great part of humanity would have willingly given their approval to the uncontrolled invention of such images" (12: 371) The outcome of the struggle is represented in Osiris as lord of the underworld, that is, Typhon is

placed in obscurity by Osiris, for in itself, that is, returned
to obscurity, the first potency is the same as the second,
Typhon is Osiris (12: 375). Consciousness is guided by
Osiris. Isis becomes queen of the realm of the dead, but not
before she leaves behind Horos, her son, as lord of the
world above (12: 376). Horos as a child in the bosom of Isis
is the characteristic image of Egyptian consciousness still
looking toward the future (12: 378). Thus, the story [*Geschichte*] of the struggle is never concluded, but is repeated
every year. "The whole of Egyptian religion remains, as it
were, a continual struggle against the Typhonic; it is the
ever recurring story of true and effective redemption." (12:
388) At certain times, Typhon, who was in a struggle with
death, was appeased by sacrifice, at other times, he was
ridiculed. And "this scorn itself is proof that consciousness
had experienced Typhon's power as a reality" (12: 387f.).
(In the same way, the Greeks mocked Kronos, and used his
name as a term of abuse for all feebleminded men [12:
388].) Egyptian mythology corresponds to the stage of animal life in nature. "The beasts, whom no thoughtful man
can consider without a certain horror, are precisely manifestations of the blind spirit of nature, which is just beginning
to attain spirituality." (13: 402) In Egyptian mythology,
which progressed from a triad of gods to the one god
(Osiris) in three forms, and hence to monotheism, there is
a clear indication of the ascent from the real gods of ordi-
nary consciousness, to the intelligible, and to that extent
unmythological and metaphysical gods of a priestly theology. These gods are unbegotten and immortal, whereas the
gods of mythology have actually come into being. The intelligible gods are Amon, who remains hidden, and who
meditates on himself; Ptah, the demiurge; Knepf, who re-
stores unity. Over against them all is Hermes Trismegistos,
that is, the consciousness that differentiates them and once

more comprehends their unity (12: 414). That the priests succeeded in impressing these gods so effectively upon folk consciousness, and that the most colossal of Egyptian edifices were built for them, is testimony of the high level of religious consciousness attained here (12: 393).

ii. India—Brahma, Shiva, Vishnu

In Indian mythology, the real principle is pushed completely into the past. It appeared in Brahma, that forgotten god who lacks images and temples, and who is scarcely worshiped any longer. But this principle is the basis of religious consciousness. Hence, in Indian mythology the characteristic religious principle has been almost entirely abandoned. This weakness of religious consciousness is evident everywhere. It appears among those who "know only how to avoid what ought not to be and yet is, but who do not know how to adjust their strings to make chords that would sound the harmony of a completely implemented science. Among them, therefore, religious consciousness is like an uncertain foreboding or yearning; it is led astray by vague and uncertain sounds" (12: 441f.). Shiva, "the god of the universal orgy," dominates common Indian consciousness (12: 444). He is the destructive principle, but not in an evil sense: he destroys Brahma, who is the power of the real principle that keeps man in bondage. The gods of popular polytheism, foremost of whom is Indra, take the place of Brahma, who has perished. They are posited by Shiva along with the dismemberment of consciousness at the nadir of the mythological process.

The unity destroyed by Shiva is restored by Vishnu. His worship is limited to the highest castes and takes the form of an abstract spiritualism. But since consciousness cannot sustain itself at such intellectual and spiritual heights it descends, according to doctrines of incarnations, to the material realm. Now, however, the assumption of material forms appears to be voluntary (12: 460). The particular incarnations of Vishnu belong more to folklore than to mythology. The most important result of the dismemberment of Indian consciousness is the spiritualistic mysticism of Vedanta. It is a purely spiritual attempt to regain unity with God beyond the potencies—a unity that had been materially destroyed. The goal of mysticism is the return of the individual soul to the absolute (12: 479). The present world is deemed to be an illusion. Maya stretches out her net of appearances before the creator, who, as it were, in a moment of self-forgetfulness, allows himself to be lured into the creation by the seductive beauty of this world (12: 482). "This is indisputably the highest point to which Idealism, that is, the belief in the mere transient and phenomenal reality of this world, could ascend without special revelation"[3] (12: 482). Just as the material aspect of mythology disappears in Indian consciousness, so does the Indian himself become more soul than body. Here, therefore, there is a strong disregard for life, and a high regard for voluntary death and asceticism, all in sharp contrast to the Egyptians and their efforts to immortalize bodily existence. Egyptian and Indian mythology are related as body and soul, but spirit transcends both, and to it corresponds Greek mythology.

iii. Greece—Hades, Poseidon, Zeus

Man is the end of the mythological as well as of the natural process. "In the history of the mythological process, [the Greek Gods] represent that moment in the history of nature following the terrible war in the animal kingdom, when the principle of nature died the calm, enchanting, truly divine death in man—as though it were an atonement for all nature. For in man all of nature is reconciled" (13: 406). Thus Greek mythology (according to Schelling, Roman mythology has no significance apart from the Greek) contains all the elements of the mythological process in perfect harmony. It stands on the same level with Egyptian and Indian mythology, inasmuch as all three are complete mythologies. But it transcends both, inasmuch as the third, spiritual potency is realized in it. Greek mythology is built upon the triad of Hades, Poseidon, and Zeus. Hades, the real principle, who is set in the past, is the lord of death, before whose dwelling even the gods shudder. For if he were to come forth the multitude of gods would disappear (13: 407). Poseidon is the real god, who is self-materializing and who surrenders to conquest. Hence liquid is his element, especially the sea, whose savagery and inner strife express Poseidon's unwilling obedience to Zeus (12: 581). Finally there is Zeus, the god, in whom all the Greeks are one, for "Greek life and being first begin with him" (12: 590). He is the chief of the multitude of gods, the truly human spiritual god.

Schelling's view of Greek mythology is based upon an analogy with the natural process. The original natural process culminates in the world of ideas. And "the Greek gods arise out of consciousness that is gently and lawfully released from the real principle as a class of blessed visions and apparitions. To be sure, in these visions, the real principle disappears, but in its disappearance and dissolution it still contributes reality and definiteness to the emerging forms. Through its effect, the Greek gods represent necessary, eternal, and abiding, rather than merely transient moments (i.e., concepts)" (13: 406). The Greek gods are ideas.

Schelling already had expressed these thoughts very clearly in his platonic period in connection with the philosophy of art. The gods of Greek mythology are for art what the ideas are for philosophy: the objects of natural intuition. Mythology is the common source of art and philosophy. But whereas at that time Schelling perceived the ideal of the future in the reunification of the three [potencies], now he regards their separation as the necessary conclusion of mythology generally. For when the world of ideas arises in consciousness, consciousness is set free from the potency of the beginning. But on account of the fall of the world of ideas, mankind has ceased to be only consciousness. The world of ideas has only ideal significance. Intellectual intuition cannot change the actual condition of the world and redeem the idea. The spirituality of Greek culture is immediate and natural, as it was with the original ideal man. But ever since that immediacy was destroyed by the self-positing act it cannot, as such, be restored. The world that has come into existence outside of God by an act of will cannot return to God by a natural process that is bound to necessity. To be sure, in Greek mythology, the false religious principle of antiquity has been exorcised and relegated to the past. However, because the reality of religious consciousness depends upon this principle, the special substance of mythology is lost with it in the deep (12: 646). Mythology merges with the rational process and culminates with it in intellectual intuition (see below). Consequently, the position of Greek culture can be characterized as follows: The power of the false pagan principle over consciousness is overthrown, but so is every real religious relationship along with it. A purely ideal relationship takes its place, which conceals within itself the postulate of a truly real religious relationship.

III. The Conclusion of the Mythological Process: The Greek Mysteries

1) In the Greek mysteries mythology attained self-consciousness, that is, it became conscious of its limits. The mysteries stand in complete correlation with the mythological consciousness of the Greeks. Because Greek mythology was the culmination of the mythological process, it reached self-consciousness in the mysteries; and because Greek mythology recognized its limits in the mysteries, in them consciousness became free from the mythological process.

Demeter represents the transition from mythology to the mysteries. She is the wife of Poseidon, and as such represents consciousness as it vacillates between Hades and Zeus. Unable to resist for long the assaults of the liberating god, she comes to recognize that her bond to the real god is something contingent, something essentially redeemable. To speak mythologically: Demeter posits an independent being, Proserpina, whose destiny is to revert to the real god. But because Demeter herself once belonged to him, this separation is not without suffering. It is experienced as rape. Demeter is the grieving, angry mother who will not be consoled by the multitude of gods who have replaced the real god. Thus far the form of Demeter belongs to mythology (13: 412). The theme of the mysteries is the reconciliation of Demeter by the birth of the highest god, the threefold Dionysos, who has replaced the multitude of gods. In the three forms of Dionysos the three potencies enter consciousness as causes of the mythological process. In his first form, Dionysos is Zagreus, the savage god who demands human sacrifice. But for Greek consciousness, he already exists in the past. His wife is Proserpina. The second Dionysos is Bacchos. He is the

liberating god of the mythological process. In the mysteries, he is Demeter's husband. But he cannot comfort her.
Indeed, he is the cause of the multitude of gods. He is the
Dionysos of the present. Finally, in the third Dionysos,
Iacchos, mythological consciousness comes to rest. Demeter is reconciled. Iacchos is the god of the future, and is
represented as a child in the bosom of Demeter. Corresponding to him is Kore, the feminine divinity, who is the
expression of the consciousness that depends upon him.
She is the heavenly Persephone, just as Iacchos is the heavenly, spiritual Zagreus. The marriage of Iacchos and
Kore is the most important festival of the mysteries.
Through it, consciousness breaks away entirely from the
necessity of the mythological process "and a new world
begins, represented, however, only in the deepest secret
of the mysteries . . . as something in the future" (13:
488).

2) The subject of the mysteries is "the history of religious consciousness, or, objectively put, the history of God
himself, whose original unspirituality has been overcome
and transfigured until it reaches perfect spirituality" (13:
494). This is conceived not as abstract doctrine, but as
actual history set forth in an objective sequence of events.
The mysteries did not teach an abstract monotheism, nor
did they combat polytheism, as did the philosophical
schools, in an unhistorical manner. The monotheism of the
mysteries overcame polytheism intrinsically. In the mysteries, monotheism was presupposed (13:501). Only in this
way could the mysteries claim equality with philosophy.
The same holds true for ethics. The mysteries did not teach
abstract ethics. Rather, initiates into the mysteries were led
gradually through genuine inner experiences from the
depths of doubt and death to the heights of blessedness
and freedom. "To be sure, the mysteries looked for libera-

tion from the material realm, but primarily from the material form of mythology. The blessedness that was won through initiation was such that the initiates, set free by it from the necessity of the mythological process, were placed in immediate communication with purely spiritual gods" (13:453). Belief in immortality was directly connected with transcending the material realm. Nevertheless, the special content of the mysteries cannot be found in it.

3) Although polytheism was now conquered in the mysteries, they made no assault upon it. For it was the absolute secret of the mysteries, whose disclosure warranted the death penalty, that a spiritual religion of the future was posited in them, a religion that could be united with the lordship of Zeus in the present. The state and the whole order of life was founded upon the exoteric gods. Therefore prophecy of their decline was interpreted as an assault upon the state. Because he stood between a public religion to which he was subject for the present and a purely spiritual religion that would appear to him in the future, a profoundly tragic tension pervaded the whole religious life of the Greek. It was "the awareness . . . that all this splendor would someday be extinguished, and this beautiful world of appearances would disappear and give way to a higher clarity without deceit and delusion" (13: 517, *sic.*). Thus Aeschylos had Prometheus say of Zeus: "He does not rule the gods for long . . . he rules the new gods for a short time only and thinks, 'your citadel is not to be conquered' " (13: 510, *sic.*). "Prometheus is the idea by which the human race, after it has brought forth the whole world of the gods from within itself, returns to itself and becomes conscious of itself and of its special fate" (11: 482) "This awareness of its necessary end brings the mythological life to a close. . . . As far as it was possible within itself, the reconciliation

of mythology occurred in the quiet of that solemn night where the Greek becomes aware of the necessary impermanence of mythological images . . . in the quiet of that night and in the solemnity of its thought" (13: 529f.).

IV. Submythological and Antimythological Elements in Mythology

1. Gods and Idols

Obviously the construction of the history of religion given here comprehends only a fraction of the religions that actually exist. But for a systematic construction, this is of no consequence. What matters here is the process by which the spiritual potency becomes predominant in consciousness. In principle, it is enough if it has been realized at one point in history. Only the quality of the outcome is valid here. As in nature, so also in history, God's way goes from the broad to the narrow. Moreover, it should be noted that his construction confines itself to the Near East and the Mediterranean region (with the sole exception of India, whose special position in the history of mythology is most comparable to Christianity). The nations of these regions and their culture are entirely interlaced with the history of Israel, and together they flow into the Hellenistic culture of the Roman Empire. Therefore an external economy is attained here that puts the concept of the "fullness of time" in a new light: when Christianity enters the world, its way is prepared in a positive sense not only by the religious history of Israel, but also by the history of paganism.

Nevertheless, in an explication of the mythological process it is necessary to explain also those phenomena that are remote from its primary development, but which far

surpass it quantitatively. For this purpose, Schelling distinguishes between gods and idols. "There are no idols in the
original theogonic consciousness. In the gods that arise
spontaneously within it, consciousness always intends and
wills only the living God. But as soon as the moment of the
first living generations of the gods is past and the representations of the gods remain as offspring of what is no longer
present, then they become idols"[4] (12: 297) This is already
the case at the moment when original Zabism leaves behind
as a residue mere material star-worship (12: 296). It applies
to fetishism, that is, the worship of inorganic substances,
which is Kronos worship that has lost its vitality (12: 294f.).
When, in the mythological process, Kronos's moment was
past, his worship became meaningless, and the nations that
remained with him became separated from history. It is a
complete mistake to confuse the nations that have fallen
out of history with the prehistorical condition of mankind
and to put fetishism at the beginning of the process (12:
296).

2. Manifestations of Reaction

a. China

Reactions against the mythological process originate
from the sense of oppression that overcomes consciousness when the god of the second potency approaches intent
of overthrowing the peaceful and undisputed sovereignty
of the first potency. The first of these reactions appears
among the Chinese, that is, that part of original humanity
which came to a standstill before the rise of mythology and
the formation of the races. At the stage of the mythological
process when universal necessity prevailed, there was only
one way to avoid onslaught of the spiritual god: by thrust-
ing the real principle out of the religious sphere into an-

other (12: 524). Thus, among the Chinese, the state took the place of god, and it retained all the attributes which, in Zabism, heaven, that is, Uranos, possessed: *Religio astralis in rem publicam versa* is the essence of Chinese culture, which "like the heaven, is immutable and unmoving" (12: 531). "By overturning the religious principle and secularizing it, Chinese consciousness spared itself entirely from the religious process. With equal originality, it attained that standpoint of pure rationality which other races reached only through the mythological process" (12: 539). The symbolic dragon and the ancestor cult were born of an awareness of that revolution into irreligion by which the heavenly realm became earthly (12: 540).

b. Parsiism

The second important appearance of reaction occurs within the mythological process itself, during the epoch of Urania. Whereas among the rest of the races, consciousness was divided between the first and second god, among the Persians, Zoroaster's movement combined both gods in the unity of the universal god, Mithras (12: 210). In his original unity, Mithras is neither expansion nor contraction, neither light nor darkness, neither the friend nor the destroyer of the creature (12: 223). The opposition between Ohrmazd and Ahriman, whose conflict informs Persian consciousness, did not arise until Mithras materialized himself out of love for the creature. In the *Zend Avesta* this conflict is conceived in a thoroughly practical sense. These books contain no speculation, only moral instruction. The characteristic Mithras idea, that is, Mithras as mediator and redeemer, belongs to the mysteries (12: 213). Therefore, the popular conception of Parsiism as an absolute dualism is false. A dismemberment of consciousness so complete and barely conceivable is neither found in the *Zend Avesta* nor inferred from the teachings of Mithras. The very idea is refuted by the promise of the final victory of Ohrmazd. Indeed, "how is the struggle possible at all if [Ohrmazd and Ahriman] are not somehow one, if they are absolutely separate, if they are not absolutely compelled to be *uno eodemque loco*" (12: 219). The Persian system is pantheistic, that is, it is an attempt to preserve monotheism that is mixed with polytheism. As a historical system, pantheism is retarded polytheism (12: 233).

c. Buddhism

Buddhism is a manifestation of the Mithras-idea appearing at a later stage of the mythological process (12: 506). Moreover, it is to be interpreted as a direct historical descendant of the Mithras-idea. The Indian race is that branch of Indo-Persian stock which abandoned the mythological process and from whose womb the original antimythological nature was brought forth at a time of the greatest confusion (12: 509). Like Mithras, Buddha is the universal god who stands solitary and alone. He "presupposes nothing outside himself . . . for he is his own substance" (12: 499f.). Nevertheless, Buddhism is not abstract pantheism. The Buddhist idea of incarnation contains a dualism within itself. The ascetic, monastic tendency in practical Buddhism also presupposes it (12: 502). The justification for regarding Buddhism as a manifestation of reaction depends, among other reasons, on the impossibility of deriving it directly from Indian mythology. It is impossible to derive Buddhism from Indian mythology because of the antithesis of spiritual, mystical Hinduism and materialistic Buddhism. The Hindu doctrine of creation separates the creator from the world, and the world never attains true being. In Buddhism, God materializes himself, and wanders throughout all the forms of nature on account of his love of the creature. He does not remain outside the creature, as does the creator according to Vedanta (12: 482).

There is evidence of an earlier influence of Buddhism on Hinduism. The Vaishnavite epics that tell of the incarnations of Vishnu reveal the influence of Buddhism (12: 517). The development of an extremely mystical and spiritualistic tendency in Vaishnavism is especially due to Buddhism. Thus, over against a fragmented polytheism, there arose in India both a materialistic and an idealistic pantheistic reaction, each in extreme opposition to the other. Buddhism was finally defeated and was driven out of India, its motherland. It spread widely among the Mongolian nations as well as among the Chinese, where it became a religion lacking a religious principle. God is without form because his unchangeable unity is beyond all the phenomena that he enters. The highest goal of man is to participate in nirvana, where God himself is. Nirvana "is usually translated as nothingness, but it really means freedom from all external being" (12: 520).

Buddhist pantheism and Hindu pantheism are also retarded polytheisms. But whereas in Persia the potencies were abruptly juxtaposed, and pantheism gave shelter to a harsh dualism, the unity of Buddhism was under the predominance of the real principle; it became pantheism in a strict sense. The unity of Hinduism was under the predominance of the second potency; it became pantheism with a deistic aspect. All three forms of pantheism are characterized by the fact that they presuppose the separation of the potencies and strive for a unity that is immediate and natural but is not free and spiritual as is the unity of monotheism. However, immediacy is destroyed on account of the Fall, and can only be restored ideally. Therefore, these pantheistic reactions, dualistic Parsiism excepted, lack the full reality of the religious relationship as it is manifest in mythology. Thus they come into close relationship with the rational process, in whose course of development pantheism reaches completion and catastrophe.

V. The Rational Process

1) The task of rational philosophy is to investigate that which is, potentiated threefold [*das dreifach potenzierte Seiende*], in all the possible combinations of the potencies with one another. It must continue its investigation until it has overcome every indeterminacy and every possibility that is still concealed, and until it reaches being as an ultimate principle that precedes all thought and is not bound by any potency (11: 560). By actualizing principles that are mere possibilities, negative philosophy develops a series of objects and their respective sciences whose status and task it defines (see below). After the potencies are deduced from the intellectual intuition of the concept of being, and the possibility of a process is perceived in the ambiguous character of the first potency, rational philosophy assumes that this possibility is realized, and the philosophy of nature reflects upon the unfolding process of realization. The ambiguity of the outcome of the philosophy of nature, of man as a natural being, leads to the assumption of the Fall, and with it, a new process in human consciousness, the cultural process. According to this construction the cultural process is nothing but the mythological process viewed from a specific standpoint. Whereas the mythological process is the history of God-consciousness, the rational process is the history of world-consciousness. But since the potencies that are effective in the world process are the same as those that dominate religious consciousness, a perfect correlation takes place between them.[xxi] All progress toward the attainment of freedom from the real potency is at the same time progress in the conscious attitude toward nature and human society, and *vice versa*.

2) The presupposition of the rational process is original man's conception of himself as an individual being, that is,

"actualized selfhood" whose realization is the multitude of separate, individual, self-positing egos. Every ego stands under the law of selfhood, of self-affirmation. In fact, the ego is nothing but self-affirmation. Therefore it experiences no constraint as such, but enjoys the proud sentiment of unobstructed freedom. It is this way among the nomads, whose way of life agrees with the stars they worship, combining a perfectly self-satisfied singularity with an absolute depencence on the law of motion. He feels free who is without duality, whose being and the law of whose being are one. But demand and obligation bring duality (12: 183). Demand enters consciousness whenever the intelligible order reacts against the state of absolute unreason by means of the moral law. The demand proves that the goal of the rational process is not the individual, but ideal or universal man, that is, the living unity of a harmoniously graded multitude to which not the individual but the whole fully corresponds (11: 529). Empirically, this law imposes itself by force. It "permits no one to transgress the bounds of the law that has been set for him. In this way it becomes possible for everyone to exercise his will for the first time" (11: 528). The state is "the law that has become actual power; it is the response to that deed by which man has set himself outside reason; it is reason in history" (11: 533). This stage in the rational process, that is, the realization of the state, takes place in the original mythological process, inasmuch as the state is borne by nations. The oppressive power of the state and the public religion that is bound inseparably to it keeps religion in original paganism within the boundaries of the nation and does not allow freedom to arise there. Liberation from the predominance of the selfish principle, which lives in consciousness as a sense of freedom, can occur only by means of a power that outwardly destroys individuality, and that brings along with it a sense of coercion. Under the protection of the power of the state, a conscious, free, and spiritual attitude toward the natural potencies develops in inner correlation with the progress of mythology. It gives rise to values that raise the individual above the state. The state becomes known in its purely external significance for the restoration of ideal humanity. This ideal came into being once in each of three great forms of the state in antiquity: Oriental despotism, Greek democracy, and Roman monarchy (11: 541ff.). Thus this construction of the rational process cannot remain at a standstill; it progresses toward an inward and individual relationship to the law that breaks through the barriers of national culture. "No one becomes the property of the state, but everyone belongs unconditionally to the moral law" (11: 553) But now it can be clearly seen "what happened to the ego when it escaped from God. . . . Its initial and natural attitude is hatred and rebelliousness toward the law. . . . For, being universal and impersonal, the law cannot avoid being harsh. . . . Whoever wills to be himself shall see himself subject to the universal" (11: 554). Thus there can be no joy, and the ego, completely discouraged, begins "to realize the nothingness and the worthlessness of his entire existence" (11: 556).

3) A turning point is reached at the moment when the curse of the law becomes known: "The possibility exists for the ego not to annul itself in its unholy situation outside God, but nevertheless to annul its active nature, to renounce its selfhood." "With this step from the active to the contemplative life, the ego also comes over to the side of God. Without knowing God it seeks a godly life in this ungodly world. And because this quest takes place in conjunction with the abandonment of selfhood, the ego regains its connection with God, for on account of its selfhood it had become separated from God" (11: 556). The

transition described here occurs in three stages: mystical, quietistic piety; aesthetic intuition; and contemplative science culminating in intellectual intuition (11: 557f.). Now once more the ego possesses God and, in him, an ideal by means of which it becomes free from itself. "But the ego has only an ideal relationship to this God . . . for contemplative science leads only to God who is the goal, therefore not to the God who actually is . . . not to the living God who is near" (11: 559). This is as far as ancient philosophy progresses: the νοησις νοησεως [xxii] is its highest definition of the divine essence that is accordingly απρακτος τας εξω πραξεις.[xxiii] If it could remain in the contemplative life, the ego might find refuge with this merely ideal God. "But the ego must be permitted to act . . . and with that the former despair returns, for its duality is not annulled" (11: 559f.). It is not annulled because the act by which potential will becomes actual will cannot be taken back. Everything that happens in this estranged world is nothing else but the realization of that act of will. But the mystical intuitive relationship to God rests upon the immediate apprehension of the divine in the finite, which indeed was justified in the original order of nature in which God was immediately realized in the process of nature. But ever since the potencies of nature received a reality outside God, leaving that original world with only an ideal significance, nature has been unable to guide the ego to the divine itself. "This is the ultimate crisis: That God who has at last been found is excluded from the idea, and himself forsakes rational science" (11: 566). That which truly is, is more than the idea, κρειττον του λογου. [xxiv] This is what the ego demands: "It wants to have Him, and Him only, the God who acts, who is providential, who being himself actual can oppose the actuality of the Fall, in short, the ego desires Him who is Lord of being" (11: 556). "For person desires person"; it does not want a God who is confined to the idea, "in which it cannot stir." Rather, the ego desires a God "who is outside of and above reason, to whom is possible what is impossible to reason, who is equal to the law, that is, a God who can set one free from the law" (11: 566f.). The ego finds its salvation only when it possesses God in actuality, and when it is united (reconciled) to him, that is, when it is united to him by means of religion, that is, by means of a voluntary, spiritual, personal religion that brings the old world in its entirety to an end (11: 567). The catastrophe of the rational process is the true end of paganism.

B. REVELATION

I. Judaism and Mohammedanism

1) Throughout the world-historical process the second potency is active: the elevation of the first potency is the starting point of the process, the realization of the third potency is the goal, but activity belongs only to the second. Just as it is necessary to distinguish in the concept of God between nature in God and the divine Self, so it is also necessary to distinguish between logos as cosmic potency and logos as personality within God. To be sure, at the conclusion of the original natural process both aspects of the logos were in perfect harmony, for God was realized in the unity of the potencies. But on account of the Fall and the separation of the potencies, nature has come to exist outside God, and in this externality the second potency has also come to dwell. At the same time, the second potency pursues God-estranged being in order to unite with it and to lead it back to God. In this process, the logos, according

to its nature, operates as cosmic potency. On the other hand, the spiritual, personal unity of the three potencies within God is undisturbed by the Fall, for this unity is nothing else but the eternal spirituality of God who posits himself in a threefold act of will. Ever since God's self-unfolding in the process of creation, his unity has evolved from eternal identity to a free and indestructible community of love.

Revelation is the term for the action of God as personality, or, since it is the logos who acts, it is the term for the action of the logos as personality within God. "The true Son, the personality that is hidden in the purely natural potency . . . is the cause of revelation in the same way as he, as purely natural potency, is the cause of all mythology" (14: 88). "There is a twofold history of the mediating potency; there is, as it were, a *historia sacra* and a *historia profana* of its action" (14: 119). The Old Testament contains the *historia sacra.* Whereas it is the task of the *historia profana* to set forth the universality of the potencies, it is the task of the *historia sacra* to reveal their unity. The former is secular for it is based on a natural process that is external to God. The latter is sacred for it is based on a supernatural process within God. The former presupposes the separation of the potencies outside God, the latter, the unity of personality within God.

2) The personal action of the logos in Judaism is conditioned, in its mode, by the state of consciousness that revelation presupposes, that is, by the relative monotheism of the beginning of the mythological process. "The *terminus a quo,* the starting point, is the same for that part of mankind with whom, we believe, the mediating potency has entered into a personal relationship, as it is for the greater part of mankind, with whom it has a purely natural relationship" (14: 120). In Israel, too, the immediate content of con-

sciousness is the God of a one-sided monotheism. Revelation occurs in this way: through the mediation of the second potency, the true God reveals himself to consciousness, which posits God in substance. God reveals himself within this substance. Therefore, this substantial, natural content of original consciousness always remains the basis and medium of revelation. This is so to the extent that, according to its natural drives, Israel passed through almost all the stages of polytheism, and revelation was in constant conflict with it. The people, even their leaders, experienced this conflict as cultural deprivation when they were not permitted to follow the gods of a later, more sophisticated age. They believed that they were held back by a past that was culturally inferior. And, indeed, as the Rechabites and the Nazarites prove, they were correct. "It is an enduring characteristic of the people of God that they were compelled to seek the builders of their temple among the Phoenicians" (11: 239). From this we can understand how strongly Israel was tempted toward polytheism. "The substance of their consciousness is thoroughly pagan; true religion was only accidental to it, that is, no more than what was revealed to their consciousness" (14: 143). Not until the Babylonian captivity did the danger of polytheism disappear, for just at that time the mythological process had lost its power among mankind generally, because its goal had been reached (14: 144).

3) A typical example of how the pagan principle, which is the basis of Judaism and which gives it reality, is governed by revelation and becomes potential through it, is the story of the sacrifice of Isaac. Elohim commands Abraham to sacrifice his son, as Kronos commanded the Phoenicians. To Abraham, this command has complete reality. But the angel of Jehovah prevents him from carrying it out. Jehovah, whom the angel manifests, is a definite

and distinct God. In contrast to that nameless God of prehistory who is substance, he has a name, that is, a form (11: 163). All the biblical narratives in which Elohim reveals his name Jehovah belong here: "The name is important, because there is no knowledge of the true God without difference. The worshipers of the true God are those who know his name" (11: 165) In particular, pagan substance and revelational form are traceable in the statutes and ordinances of Mosaic religion [*Mosaismus*]. Thus, circumcision is a mitigation of the religious castration cult (14: 134). The ark of the covenant and the tabernacle correspond to Egyptian prototypes (14: 136). Leading a he-goat into the wilderness to Asasel is a sacrifice to the God of the prehistoric era (14: 140). The essence of sacrifice is necessarily grounded not in revelation, but in mythology (14: 145). The statutes that prescribe sacrifice merely normalize a custom whose reality is presupposed. "Mosaic religion is inconceivable if one does not perceive within it the reality of paganism on the one hand, and actual revelation on the other" (14: 145) For revelation cannot immediately dissolve a tension that has once been posited, it can do so only through a process (14: 145) "The secret of the formation and the structure of the Old Testament is based, for the most part, upon the necessity to cherish and preserve this pagan substance" (14: 125).

4) Just as paganism reached self-consciousness in the mysteries and also transcended itself, so did Israel in Prophetism. Spirit, the potency of the future, speaks already in the prophets of Israel and leads beyond the law, without, however, annulling it for the present. To be sure, "that superstitious customs like those prescribed in the Mosaic ceremonial law" should somehow continue to develop during the age of the Kings of Israel was made impossible by the prophets (11: 174n). But just as little was the

importance of such customs for that present disputed. Prophetic universalism is to be explained in the same way. For the present it let the boundaries of the chosen race remain.

The mythological element was the foundation of the post-prophetic development of Judaism. For the Jews it became the mantle of the supernatural, and thereby holiness itself. Therefore, it was very difficult for the Jews "to free themselves from their ritual law, and from that purely cosmic element peculiar to it" (14: 149). In paganism, the purely cosmic powers became impotent in themselves through the metaphysical process. In Judaism, as the substrate of revelation, they held the power of the antitheological principle. The result was a paradox: the power of the mythological principle enjoyed its final triumph in the antimythological religion of revelation (11: 150 *sic.*).

According to this construction, the history of the religion of Israel ran through three periods: a) the normalizing through revelation of the basic mythological religious functions (in brief, the development of Mosaic religion), b) the spiritual understanding of the Mosaic law and the prophecy of the spiritual religion of the future (Prophetism), c) complete rejection of mythology, together with legal fixation of the substantial, mythological, and the formal, antimythological elements of Mosaic religion (normative Judaism).

5) The assertion that the mythological principle enjoyed its final triumph in the antimythological religion of revelation is supremely applicable to that world-historical after-effect of Judaism in Mohammedanism. The awesome successes of Mohammed can only be explained as due to "a prodigious force rising again from the past . . . which burst forth destroying and laying waste the tradition and culture that by that time had evolved" (11: 167). Just at the moment when Christianity, which not only excluded polytheism as Judaism had done, but also assimilated it, had com-

pletely overcome "the austere one-sided unity of original monotheism, the ancient, primordial religion arose once again—irrationally and fanatically—with the force of necessity" (11: 167). Mohammed set the austere, impassive god of prehistory not only against the polydaimonism prevailing among his clansmen, but above all against the apparent polytheism of Christianity. "Like the Rechabites, Mohammed even forbade his followers to take wine" (11: 168).

II. Christianity

1. The Fullness of Time

1) Paganism and Judaism both pointed beyond themselves by prophesying a perfect religion of the future; and both ended in a catastrophe that realized the negative moment of the prophecy and made the positive moment an urgent demand [Postulat]. A characterization of the "fullness of time" is nothing other than a definition of this demand. The presupposition of the history of religion prior to the advent of Christianity is the elevation of the irrational potency and its predominance over the world in opposition to the divine. Through the process of the history of religion the perversity of this presupposition becomes known, but it is not conquered. Consciousness has become free from the potency of the beginning, but it has not become lord over it. To escape from it, consciousness must take refuge in contemplation of the idea; but God is beyond the idea. And when, by an inescapable necessity, consciousness has returned to reality, it comes under the jurisdiction of that which ought not to be. Thus, the postulate of the fullness of time is twofold: negatively, deliverance from the power of the that which ought not to

be, and positively, communion with the true God. The
demand that externality to God be annulled and communion with God be established marks the end of the process
of history.[xxv]

2) This demand [*Forderung*] receives an entirely different
meaning when viewed in the light of the trinitarian relationships. The second potency obtains sovereignty over being
through the mythological process. But being, which the
logos has followed in order to unite with it, exists outside
God. Ever since the Fall, God is no longer united with his
will in being. Being, therefore, is a natural process external
to God. By means of this process, the logos becomes the
Lord of being. Thus his lordship is also external to God.
It was an act of self-sacrifice when the Son followed being
outside God in order to rescue it from destruction by divine
wrath. But this is precisely the true will of the Father, which
he cannot directly reveal on account of his righteousness.
For God wants to become reconciled to being. "However,
the fact that the Son recognizes that he is still dependent
upon the Father, and that his will is the will of the Father,
does not at all change the condition of his external inde-
pendence" (14: 38) His sovereignty is external to God. The
basis of his personality is nature, which is external to God.
Therefore he is independent of God. On the other hand,
his personality, that is, his will, is the will of God, and in this
he is independent of nature. "The nature of the true mediator is to be so situated that he is independent of both parts"
(14: 50). As mediator, the Son has entered into a relationship of *heteroousia* with the Father. He has departed from an
original *tautoosia,* for only in this way can he attain *homoousia,* that is, a free, spiritual community of persons.[xxvi]
"The moment of *heteroousia* is absolutely necessary if the
trinity is not finally to become merely nominal. Unless the
trinitarian principles have been actually autonomous, out-

side each other and opposed to each other, there is nothing
that can prevent them from becoming a merely nominal
trinity" (14: 67) The fullness of time may be characterized
as the moment of separateness, as the demand that the Son
forsake the lordship that he could have had independent of
the Father, that is, the demand that he be the Christ (13:
37).

2. The Work of Christ

"The principal benefit of Christianity was liberation from
paganism," redemption from the power of darkness, "i.e.,
from the blind power to which humanity had been subjected in paganism" (13: 184). This is the judgment of the
New Testament, that paganism was unfree and unspiritual,
and lay under the power of the cosmic potencies. Therefore, an understanding of mythology is so important, because "the reality of . . . redemption is related exactly in this
way to the power and dominion from which it liberates or
redeems us" (13: 184). The power that kept paganism in
servitude, even when consciousness had struggled free
from it, was the will of the first potency, of that infinite
subjectivity and blind selfhood which destroys the creature.
We have seen that ever since the Fall the will of God is not
directly manifest in the world. It is manifest as wrath. As
will, infinite subjectivity is supported by God. But he does
not, according to his will, approve of the tendency of that
will, of its form, of actualized selfhood and its consequences, namely, evil, death, and destruction. Insofar as he
supports and sustains it, he does so through his anger. That
which ought not to be but which has become actual is at the
same time object and subject of divine wrath. Therefore,
redemption becomes reconciliation. It is true that through
the mythological process, the second potency has become

lord of the first principle, "but, so far as it opposes that principle only as a natural or a cosmic potency . . . its conquest over it can only be external" (14: 194). The first principle is not cut off at its root; its right to be is not annulled. It is the right of this principle, aroused by man, to have the power over him to destroy him. And God's righteousness does not allow this right to be taken from it. "He is the God of this principle, as well as the God of the mediating potency which opposes it. For he is the universal God, and it is his nature to be universal." (14: 195) His divine majesty lies in the fact that he is not an exclusive principle, but universality itself.[5] "It can be said that it is God's highest law to preserve this opposing principle. For according to his primary being, it is from this principle (when he has finally overcome it) that God derives the most powerful affirmation of his divinity and sovereignty. . . . It is this principle that God makes into law, in order to overcome it intrinsically" (14: 195).

But the power and right of the potency of selfhood culminate in the destruction of the creature. Therefore, both its power and right are exhausted when it has killed him who has become lord of being, and in whom everything finite is sacrificed to the inifinite. Because Christ is the Lord of being, his death is a sacrificial death in behalf of being. Because Christ makes possible the existence of all creatures, and because all life is comprehended within him, so that light is wrought out of darkness, therefore his death signifies the complete exhaustion of the principle of darkness (14: 203). The power of darkness, which was unleashed by the Fall, possesses the right of divine wrath against that victorious potency which had reached the summit of natural and spiritual dominion over the principle of nature at the end of the pagan period. The power of selfhood was shattered upon the self-sacrifice and self-surrender of all lordship external to God, upon the personal act of the logos, which surpasses all that is natural.[6]

Now God is again related to the world as Father. Once again he can affirm man completely, for Christ in his resurrection has been clothed forever with human existence "as proof that human nature is again justified and completely acceptable to God" (14: 217). "Therefore we have received the gift of *justification* . . . and our present condition of separateness from God becomes one in which God acknowledges us, and in which we can live in peace and joy" (14: 218). In Christ, original man, that is, ideal man, is also restored (14: 219). For just as the Fall was the elevation of selfhood, so redemption is the sacrifice of selfhood. And all who sacrifice their self-will with Christ enter through him and in him into the unity of love: a unity that is higher than the original, immediate unity, as high above it as spirit is above nature: *it is the communion of Saints whose head is Christ.* The positive aspect of all of these consequences of the redemptive work of Christ can be summarized by the assertion that communion with the true God has been restored, that is, communion with the personal divine self, who is more than the idea, and who is therefore able to come forth from·the idea, who, as personal, can draw what is personal to himself. This is what mankind, conscious of his separateness, demanded [*postulierte*] at the end of the rational process. In mythical forms God was perceived as nature, for man was related only to the cosmic potencies. In Christ the divine self is revealed as a spiritual personality who acts historically and who breaks through all the limitations of nature. *This, then, is the content of all of history: the work of Christ, namely, to sacrifice his natural being in order to find himself again in spirit and in truth; this is the content of history because it is the essence of Spirit.* In Christ and through Christ we receive God as Spirit. *In* Christ, because in him who is historical personality, the historical, personal God meets man. *Through Christ*, because through his self-denial, death, and glorification, the Spirit is realized. This leads to the final, highest, and comprehensive effect of the work of Christ. As long as the predominance of the ideal principle was external to God and cosmic, only a cosmic and natural spirit could appear. Only when the first potency has been denied its right, and has been conquered at the root of its being, that is, morally, and only when, by means of this conquest, the tension of the potencies has been completely dissolved, can the Holy Spirit, "the Spirit who is from God," and therefore the Spirit of freedom, regain predominance over being (14: 237). "But the Gospel is the perfect law of freedom whereby the external law, the external necessity that underlay all consciousness, is annulled. In Christ the whole cosmic religion died" (14: 239). *We have the Spirit. This distinguishes Christianity from all other Religions.* And we have him because he has been brought to us by the work of Christ, because through him the tension of the potencies has been dissolved in God himself and the unity of all has been realized with absolute perfection. Therefore, Christianity is necessarily monotheism, or community with the triune God.

3. *The Development of the Church*

At the conclusion of his lectures on the philosophy of revelation Schelling presented a construction of the history of the Church in three periods designated by the three apostles, Peter, Paul, and John.[xxvii] Peter, the real, relatively unfree principle, governs Catholicism. Paul, in whom dwells the ideal, liberating potency, corresponds to Protestantism, "which, however, only mediates the transition to a third period," in which John, the spiritual potency, rules.

The view of Church history in the *Exposition of the Philosophy of Pure Reason*[xxviii] is very much better than this schematic construction. In this work, the goal of the historical development of the Church is represented as the realization of free or philosophical religion. There can no longer be any doubt in what sense Christianity is free religion in contrast to mythology. "But Christianity only mediates free religion, it does not immediately posit it. . . . As the negation of paganism and in its opposition to it, Christianity becomes effective by becoming real, incomprehensible power. . . . In opposition to the power that remains external to it, Christianity must also become external and blind power for a while" (11: 258f.) The power of Catholicism is the power that Christianity took away from paganism and kept for itself. The Renaissance marks the beginning of liberation from this power. The antithesis of Christianity and paganism was relaxed, as the uninhibited reception of classical paganism demonstrates. But the process could not end here because paganism had long before penetrated the Church in Christian forms. As a result there came next, in the Reformation, a reaction against everything pagan. It was marked by a turning away from tradition and a return to the original documents of revelation. But as a result consciousness fell into a new servitude, inasmuch as the authority of those "[written] monuments which originated under casual conditions without the force of necessity" could not bind consciousness internally (11: 260). Moreover, this authority held sway for only a short time. Reason is the source of the final and definitive liberation. Its way was prepared by the rationalism that originated in the Aristotelian metaphysics of Scholasticism.[7] "But consciousness that has fled from revelation has recourse only to natural knowledge which does not increase freedom, and to natural reason which, as the Apostle says, learns nothing from the

Spirit of God, but is only formally and externally related to the divine. Therefore, consciousness has recourse only to another necessity, to another law, and to more presuppositions, namely, those of its unrealized capability for knowledge" (11: 260). Rationalists have no justification to call themselves, among other things, free thinkers (11: 260n). "For, as before, consciousness was destined to be free from revelation, so it was destined once again to be free from natural reason" (11: 263). It was Kant's deed to have accomplished this liberation. As Hamann said of Socrates, Schelling said of Kant's *Critique:* "The seed of corn of our wisdom must die and must disappear in unwisdom, so that from this death and this nothingness the life and being of a higher knowledge may spring forth and be created anew" (11: 255, *sic.*). At this point, Schelling expresses in a classic way the significance of the religious self-consciousness of German Idealism for the history of philosophy: It is the consciousness that guides the liberating power of Christianity to its perfect outcome. It is fundamental to the dialectical method (see above) that nothing external or untelligible, and, therefore, servile, be tolerated, not even religion. But one must become ignorant and immature and begin at the beginning in order to make a beginning with the unconditioned, with freedom. Everything conditioned enslaves, only the unconditioned, the act, makes free. Mythology is a process, therefore it enslaves. Revelation is a free act, therefore it sets free. "But by overcoming unspiritual religion intrinsically, revelation sets consciousness in opposition to it in freedom, and in this way mediates free religion, the religion of the Spirit, which, because its nature is to be sought and found only with freedom, can be realized completely only as philosophical religion" (11: 255). Philosophical religion contains no more factors than do mythology and revelation. But it contains them as concepts, and therefore opposes them in freedom. Just as God's freedom is such that he is free from his being as Spirit, so man also must be free from a one-sided restriction to spiritual religion. The perfection of spiritual religion lies in the fact that it can be free even from itself, free for the eternally valid results of the mythological process: art and science, state and culture. The Renaissance could not accomplish this, because it knew only a pagan reason that opposed revelation as soon as it was given the opportunity. Only by uniting with the Reformation did reason free itself from its natural restrictions and discover in Idealism the freedom that Christianity had brought. Therefore, philosophical religion will arise from Idealism, which comprehends God as nature and God as Spirit in the same freedom: for God is the one and universal God.

PART III. THE RELIGIO- AND HISTORICO-PHILOSOPHICAL PRINCIPLES OF THE CONSTRUCTION OF THE HISTORY OF RELIGION

I. The Concept of Religion

1. *Methodological Considerations*

1) There are no separate discussions about the method leading to a concept of religion in Schelling's work. Nevertheless, is it not difficult to recognize from the presentation of his philosophy the method that he actually follows, especially since its presuppositions are clearly given in Schelling's overall philosophical outlook. These presuppositions lead at once to a triple negation. As a philosopher of religion Schelling necessarily rejects the theological method that presupposes the absoluteness of Christianity and derives the concept of religion from its absolute realization in Christianity without regard to the forms of religious life that underlie it. For the philosopher of religion, the abso-

luteness of Christianity is a problem whose solution requires a concept of religion. Schelling gives even less consideration to the empirical method, which attempts to derive the concept of religion by abstraction from the religions taken all together. Indeed, one cannot even begin this task without presupposing some concept of religion with whose help what is religious can, at the start, be distinguished from the wealth of historical phenomena. Schelling absolutely transcends this contradictory empiricism by following the requirements of the dialectical method to show that understanding every phenomenon is an expression of a necessary act of reason. In the first place, this requirement may be construed in an entirely formal way: that is, as a demand to demonstrate, following the critique of reason, a universal a priori norm for a specific group of rational acts. This methodological demand applies to logic, ethics, and aesthetics, and also in the same way to religion. Schelling, in the company of Kant, also adhered to it for a long time, without, however, establishing an independent a priori for religious phenomena. He treated religion exactly as Kant did, as a supplement to ethics. The three potencies of the ideal series are knowledge, action, and art; religion is treated under the second potency (6: 136). Art is superior to religion. And philosophy, which is the absolutely nonpotent [das absolut Potenzlose], is superior to both. Nevertheless, it should be noted that here, in contrast to Kant, the formal a priori is not set in opposition to individual contents as a universal norm. Rather, both are joined together in an uninterrupted dialectical process of subject and object. It was Fichte who took this step beyond Kant. He found that the common ground of the functions of reason, which, for Kant, stood side by side without mediation, was a principle rich in content, namely the self-positing ego that comprehended itself in the rational process.

Being, substantial spirituality, is the ground of universal norms. The dualism of an abstract norm yielding universal laws on one side, and, on the other, an individual estranged from and even hostile to norms, has been overcome. The individual finds itself in its actuality when it places itself within the substantiality of the spiritual. Nevertheless, with regard to the universal schema of the spiritual functions, one is justified in setting this Fichtean viewpoint on the same stage of development as the Kantian. For the three potencies, the theoretical, the practical, and the aesthetic, correspond exactly to the three Kantian *Critiques,* and designate the three general classes of rational acts, under which all others must be subsumed. As such, they are thoroughly formal and a priori in relation to the contents subordinate to them. Nevertheless, at one point Kant is surpassed, and this is the point of further development: it is the conception of philosophy as the absolutely nonpotent. For intellectual intuition, the organ of philosophy, is not an individual rational act like the rest, but the expression of the perfect aseity of reason, of its substantial identity with itself. When this state of affairs is conceived in a religious sense—as Schelling did on the basis of the doctrine of freedom—then the critical, formal method is completely negated. The essence of religion is not to be sought in some form of spirituality, but in the spirituality of man as such.[1]

2) To reach the essence of religion it is necessary to conceive the spirituality of man in an original and substantial relatedness to God. The method becomes speculative. Its starting point is the conception of the principles in the self-understanding of the spiritual personality.[xxix] It shows that in this self-understanding, individual subjectivity inasmuch as it is based upon a perversion of the principles, is immediately surpassed. The falsehood of individual subjec-

tivity enters consciousness together with the truth of the supra-individual spirituality. In this manner, the method ascends to the thought of God so that it may descend once more to the philosophy of nature. Finally, it reaches its goal in anthropology, at the same time justifying speculatively its starting point. Concretely, the method proceeds as follows: the individual comprehends itself as a free, spiritual unity of a subjective and an objective principle. However, at the same time it becomes aware that, empirically considered, this unity has been distorted by the predominance of the subjective principle. But since the individual knows that its characteristic truth has been comprehended by the former spirituality, it is led to an objective, supra-individual, absolute spirit in whom the principles are realized in perfect freedom and spirituality. When, in this way, the self-transcending of the individual spirit has led to the absolute spirit, it then becomes necessary to consider the descent of the absolute to the individual spirit. From a positive, empirical point of view, this is the task of the positive philosophy as the doctrine of creation; from the rational point of view, it is the task of the philosophy of nature. Whereas the doctrine of creation shows that God has set the principles in tension for the sake of the creature, the philosophy of nature treats the process of the reunification of the potencies which is achieved in man. The construction has returned to its beginning and has justified its starting-point in human spirituality.[2] At the same time, however, because this thought process culminates in the idea of God, the anthropological formula becomes a formula expressing the concept of religion. The pure substance of human consciousness is by nature God-positing. Human consciousness stands in a real and substantial relationship to God, and this is the religious relationship.

3) It has been shown how the speculative method has

been derived from the critical method. Now it is necessary
to discuss their relationship to each other. The speculative
construction has, in principle, reached its goal at the end
of the natural process, and the general concept of religion
has been discovered. But man is not merely nature, he is
also spiritual being, for he has the capacity to depart from
his essential spirituality and to fall into relative unspirituality, and therefore into relative irreligiosity. But inasmuch as
he remains man, the concept of religion must remain the
same even though it is differentiated in the various religions. But now, because the condition of relative spirituality and piety allows for any number of possible combinations that cannot be defined a priori, the empirical method
becomes applicable. Once negative philosophy has established the possibility of a new separation of the potencies,
and positive philosophy has shown its actuality in the doctrine of the Fall, the concept of relative spirituality and
piety, which was deduced speculatively, can be brought to
consciousness in all its richness of content by means of the
empirical method.

The theological method also gains new significance. For
since it is characteristic of the speculative method to construct the concept of religion on the basis of the concept of
God, it would have been impossible to construct an adequate concept of religion on the basis of relative spirituality
and relative communion with God.[3] Only on the basis of
the restoration of original spirituality in absolute religion
is that spiritual self-comprehension possible which is the
beginning and end point of the entire construction. And it
must be added here also that this spiritual self-comprehension becomes possible only in that moment when consciousness has won its freedom from absolute religion, that
is, freedom that makes possible a uniform understanding of
relative and absolute religion. This is the standpoint of

philosophical religion. The concept of religion is built upon the ground of philosophical religion, and with it the construction of history comes to an end. The circle of the system that is drawn with its radius through the philosophy of history has been closed once again.[4] It is of the essence of the speculative method that the concept of religion is completed only with the completion of the system.

In the course of this methodological discussion, different forms of the concept of religion have emerged. They will now be considered in order.

2. *The Concept of Religion in General*

1) The pure substance of human consciousness is by nature God-positing. Schelling's anthropology culminates in this principle, and in it lies the seed of his entire philosophy of religion. A brief look at Schelling's philosophical development will facilitate our understanding of this principle. In the methodological discussion, our consideration of the transition from the critical to the speculative method led to the conclusion that Schelling conceived of the absolutely nonpotent as the religious. This notion was developing ever since Schelling's Fichtean period, particularly with respect to the debate concerning the practical or theoretical knowledge of God. Whereas Kant had turned against those metaphysicians who attempted to reach God through deductions, who argued that God was indispensable for an explanation of the world, Schelling struggled against Kantians who postulated God because morality cannot get along without him (5: 115). He regarded this as a relapse into dogmatism, inasmuch as God once again is made an object and his existence is theoretically formulated. But God comes into existence only when he is realized by a free act of the ego. Postulates are not directed to the theoretical

faculty so that the existence of God may be assumed on moral grounds, rather they are directed to the moral faculty, so that God may be realized by moral acts in the broadest sense (1: 333). The ego exists in its inmost freedom and action; and where it is, God is. The ego that is truly such is God-positing. But the essence of the ego is morality.

When we come to the philosophy of identity, we find that the place of action has been taken by the identity of action and rest in intellectual intuition. But, in general, Schelling's opinion remains the same: "God himself must be the substance of all thinking and acting, and not a mere object. . . . God is either generally unknown, or he is at once the subject and the object of knowledge" (6: 558). "Reason does not have the idea of God, rather it is this idea, and nothing more. . . . Just as one cannot ask the light, whence comes its brightness, because it is brightness itself, so one cannot ask reason whence comes the idea of God, because it is itself precisely this idea. . . . The idea of God is not an object of dispute or discord; all particularity, from which alone there is conflict, disappears within it. The madman who denies it unwittingly expresses it: he is unable to unite two concepts logically except in this idea" (7: 149) Fundamental to all these formulas is the notion that the essential nature òf the ego is to be God-positing; even the substance of atheistic consciousness is religious. Every doctrine of the "original atheism" of human consciousness is out of the question (12: 121). "Rather, human consciousness has, from the beginning, as it were, grown together with God. . . . Consciousness has God within itself, not as an object before it," as it later came to be expressed (12: 120). Thus, the notion is throughout the same.

Nevertheless, Schelling did not perceive in these formulations a formulation of the concept of religion. Actual religion presupposes activity and like all action belongs to the second potency. It "belongs to the free and noble spirit of man to act as God has instructed him, and, in acting, not to deviate from what knowledge has discovered. True religion is heroism. . . . They are called men of God in whom the knowledge of the divine becomes immediate through action" (6: 559). Beyond all activity, purely in itself, consciousness has its being in intellectual intuition. This is the organ of philosophy. But the more abstractly intellectual intuition was conceived, and the more it was conceived as the absolutly nonpotent in contrast to the potencies, the less cause there was to identify intellectual and philosophical intuition. For although philosophy considers relative points of indifference, it is activity, and only at the end does it attain pure intellectual intuition. Intellectual intuition, as the pure God-positing consciousness in itself, transcends all the potencies, therefore it transcends philosophy also so long as the latter has not attained its goal. But once Schelling developed the doctrine of freedom and solved the problem of the world that is estranged from the idea by means of the concept of the fall of the idea from its original God-positing substantiality, and by means of the theistic (monotheistic) conception of the doctrine of God, this original relationship, now existing in the past, was conceived as the essential religious relationship. The fact that this solution occurred at this time, is due to Schelling's feeling, which is quite correct, that the formulation of a concept of religion must necessarily include a relationship between God and man that presupposes a definite division between them. But this was impossible according to the pantheistic concept of God of the system of identity, and according to the abstract conception of intellectual intuition. In identity every distinction is dissolved. This situation was changed only by the introduction of an irrational factor within God, and by the differentiation of the divine self from his nature. Once this original identity has been fragmented, then reunification is indeed possible, but not a restoration of identity, rather, a perfect community founded upon the glorification of nature's darkness into the light of the divine self.

2) The "Positive Philosophy" does not essentially go beyond this conclusion. The religious relationship is real, because it is a communion of that which is—recapitulated in man, its central idea—with him who is that which is. The religious relationship is essentially a relationship of God with himself, as nature. Therefore it is thoroughly real and substantial. Because being, which has become itself in man, is the being of God, man is absolutely bound to God. Thus he is God-positing before all knowing and willing, and stands in a relation to him that he cannot only posit, but which he only destroys as soon as he passes over into act. "[Consciousness's] first movement is not a movement by which it seeks God, but one by which it separates itself from him" (12: 120). Here the extraordinary importance of the concept of God for the concept of religion is demonstrated. The deistic concept of God deprives religion of reality, because it deprives human consciousness of its substantial divinity. Between two substances there is no real relationship, for the identity of the real is denied together with the identity of substance. The result is an assertion of the essential atheism of human consciousness, and the reduction of the religious relationship to an accidental one, inasmuch as it is contingent upon the concept of man.[5] To the usual functions of feeling, intellect, and will, Deism adds another that is related to God, and this purely ideal relation is called religious. In this way, a temporal state of consciousness is made into a norm: a state of consciousness that emerges in the history of religions at that moment when consciousness has freed itself from the reality of the false religious princi-

ple. Schelling formed his concept of religion in protest against this standpoint.

The question remains what positive significance the three functions of reason have for the religious relationship. That any one of them is specifically religious is ruled out by the whole construction, for the pure substance of consciousness is the *prius* of every specific function of reason. On the other hand, it is easy to infer from the general concept of religion that they are all together in every actual religion in a special and indispensable way. The substance of human consciousness is naturally God-positing. Therefore, a fundamental place is assigned primarily to feeling. The reality, or substantiality, of the religious relationship manifests itself as a feeling of complete obedience towards God. The tremendous power that religious experience exercises over consciousness is founded upon a feeling of essential bondage to God. Religious feeling is a feeling of unconditional obligation toward a specific god. It can only be overcome by the most profound convulsion of consciousness, as is manifest above all in mythology, but also at many points in revelation. Whereas this feeling is the real basis of the religious relationship, thought gives it a definite expression. For religion is not a general or a formal feeling of dependence, but an awareness of obligation toward a definite God. Therefore, representations of God or concepts of God are essential constituents of religion. By means of these concepts and representations, consciousness expresses its knowledge of the mode of its dependence and the progress of the religious relationship takes place, for the God-positing principle lies within consciousness, and it is essential to it to know and to make distinctions.

Finally, the principle that consciousness is God-positing concerns the will. As God-positing, the will has the power to surpass [*aufheben*] God, to deprive him of his sovereignty over being, and therefore to destroy the normal religious relationship. By a free act the will has annulled its being within God. By the compulsion to act, the will is driven to catastrophe that brings it to an awareness of its externality to God. Community with God is spiritual and personal and is founded upon the sacrifice of the selfish will to God. In philosophical religion, that freedom is attained in which morality is perfected. Because the construction of the concept of God rests upon moral categories, religion, as a relation that is essentially within God, is inextricably and intrinsically bound to morality. Thus the concept of religion in general is defined, and its relationship to the remaining spiritual functions has been settled in principle. One cannot, of course, speak of an actual relation of the spiritual functions in the original and substantial condition of consciousness, for here identity dominates completely. Nevertheless, within this condition reside potentially all the distinctions that find their concrete expression in the actual religions.

3. *Natural Religion and Rational Religion*

1) As an introduction to the philosophy of mythology Schelling undertook a purely historical investigation of the essence and origin of mythology together with a critique of the different attempts at interpretation known to him.[xxx] He rejected, first of all, the hypothesis that poets are the originators of representations of the gods. For it is inexplicable how a universal and irresistible drive could generate a poetry that contains stories of the gods (11: 15). Moreover, although a poetic world of the gods actually appears in the earliest cultures, it reaches perfection only in Greek mythology. This interpretation of the origin of mythology

is correct only so far as it takes the mythological representations literally without, of course, attributing truth to them. Thus, it is opposed to allegorical theories, such as the euhemerist, moralistic, physicalistic, and grammatical theories that admit truth to the allegorical forms, but only in a special sense. Now it is certainly a testimony to the universality of mythology "that once allegorical interpretation is allowed, it is almost more difficult to say what [a myth] does not signify, than to say what it does signify" (11: 29). But allegorical theories cannot explain how truth might have received such a symbolic disguise without presupposing, as do most interpretations of this kind, a modern scientific consciousness. It is just as impossible to attempt to interpret mythology as fiction or invention. For a fiction created by an individual would never have been able to gain such power over nations or tribes, and the invention of a nation or tribe would presuppose the existence of nations prior to the rise of mythology. But it is precisely mythology that makes a nation a nation, or a race a race. Psychological interpretations are closer to the truth, especially the form that maintains that the representations of the gods arise from the fear of personalized natural phenomena. But this view is opposed by the fact that in all mythologies natural objects that are believed to be animated are subordinated to the gods and become their servants. "This attempt to bring forth the gods without God does not appear to have realized the true strength and power of the concept of God" (11: 73). "The fact is that this so-called religion [of fear] is only atheism combined with superstition. The objects worshipped by it have not the slightest connection with our idea of divinity"—so writes Hume, the chief advocate of this theory (11: 74). Without distinguishing between a lower and a higher level of strictly religious representations, mythology remains unexplained.

Religious methods of interpreting mythology stand on surer ground than the atheistic and nonreligious methods treated thus far. First to be considered is the evolutionary, in particular, Hegelian method that begins with a religious instinct and traces its gradual development in mythology. It has value so far as it shows that mythology originates from a necessary and purely intrinsic motivation. But this Hegelian method presupposes something that it itself has not yet comprehended, namely, that original instinct which "must be something real, an actual potency, which one could not hope to explain by means of the mere idea of God" unless, together with this method, "one first reduces the idea of God to its most paltry form, so that it can achieve perfection again through the artistry of thought" (11: 77). The problem is not one of relating the content of mythology to the idea, "but of the actual beginning of mythology." Only a positive, historical philosophy is in a position to explain this.

The monotheistic hypothesis makes an important beginning in this direction. It maintains that mythology is monotheism that has become differentiated. Montheism was imparted to an as yet undivided human race in an original revelation; then it became obscure with the rise of races and nations, and was differentiated into polytheism. However, the question remains, what caused it to become obscure? Not the division of nations, for the latter depends upon the former. Therefore, it must have been an internal process. But it is hardly clear how from unity its exact opposite, multiplicity, can proceed. Above all, the concept of original revelation is not without difficulty, for revelation is possible only where there is darkness. Whoever places revelation at the beginning presupposes, at least, an original atheism. He limits the religious interpretation of mythology to the moment of communication through revelation. The situation before and after this moment, polytheism in a strict sense, is given a nonreligious interpretation. A correct interpretation of mythology is reached by an inquiry into the essence of polytheism. A distinction must be made between primary and secondary polytheism, between belief in a succession of gods and the assumption of a multiplicity of gods existing simultaneously. The latter is not polytheism in a strict sense, because it unites the multitude of gods to a chief god who comprehends all the others in himself. Only successive polytheism is the special problem of mythology, for here multitudes of gods confined to themselves oppose and struggle against one another. Thus, Uranos, Kronos, and Zeus represent the type of successive polytheism in its purest form, whereas Zeus, together with gods governed by him, represents simultaneous polytheism in its purest form (11: 120). Now, the succession and struggle of the gods can be explained precisely by the succession of the gods in human consciousness. "Mythology, the history of the gods, therefore mythology in a strict sense, can only be produced in life itself. It must be something lived or experienced" (11: 125). But this implies that in the beginning there can only have existed a God who did not exclude the possibility of another. This was a condition of relative and not absolute monotheism. Here, the historical investigation reaches a point where it points beyond itself. For the relative monotheism of prehistory can only be explained by a supra-historical fact that is beyond the realm of historical investigation. Speculative thought has the final say about the concept of mythology.

2) According to the formulation of the general concept of religion, the reality of the religious relationship rests upon the God-positing substantiality of consciousness. But consciousness receives this character from the first potency in its potentiality, in its being-as-ground [*Basis-Sein*]. For

consciousness is the first potency that has been brought back to itself and has come to itself. Now, when the first potency again emerges from its potentiality and dominates consciousness, then the substance of consciousness is no longer God-positing as before. But also it is not absolutely godless; rather it posits the god who ought not to be, the false god. Paganism is false religion, for it presupposes the being of that which ought not to be. Nevertheless, it is actual religion, for it is founded upon a real relationship to God. In paganism, God acts together with consciousness. He does not forsake it. But the potency by which he acts is that which ought not to be, that is, the principle of his displeasure. Hence paganism is at the same time the revelation of the goodness and of the wrath of God: of goodness, insofar as he does not condemn to destruction the consciousness that opposes him; of wrath, insofar as consciousness is under the power of a false religion. This is a recurrence of Schelling's dual evaluation of nature. In nature God is both concealed and revealed: concealed, insofar as the presupposition of nature is the elevation of the first potency; revealed, insofar as without this elevation all particularity must remain in darkness. Mythology is an error, as is nature (12: 646). But the error exists in a higher potency; its presupposition is not the divine will that is lord of the potencies, but the anti-divine that wants to raise itself to be lord and falls into servitude. Its presupposition is a lie. And therefore, not only is God concealed within it, but the anti-divine is revealed; on the other hand God is revealed not only as nature, but as person. Although this two-fold highest revelation is fundamental to mythology (the logos followed God-estranged being outside God), it nevertheless does not come to light in mythology, but in revelation. The presupposition of mythology is, to be sure, something supernatural in a divine and in an anti-divine sense, but it is not this presupposition that must be over-come in [the mythological process], but rather the conse-quence of this presupposition in consciousness. Therefore, the process is yet again a natural one, and mythology is in its concept a natural religion.[6] The operation of the poten-cies is thoroughly natural. The mythological process is bound by the same necessity as the natural process. Con-sciousness would gladly escape from its movement, but it is bound to it as is nature (12: 129). The active potencies are the same as those in the natural process, and so are their products. Hence the concept of natural religion is joined to the religion of nature. God works in mythology according to his nature, not according to his heart, his personal self. Consciousness is related to God only as the potency of nature, therefore the gods of mythology are natural beings even when they have a perfect human form. They are not products of consciousness so far as it is hu-man, but rather so far as it has relapsed into a relatively prehuman stage. "Mythological representations originate exactly in this way: the past, which has already been con-quered externally in nature, enters consciousness again; that principle which has already been overcome in nature has now once more taken possession of consciousness it-self" (12: 129). "Mythology contains past times that vanish from it into human consciousness. Nature is also a history that disappears. Those scenes of sorrow and anger and of reconciliation and reassurance which we know only in this way are reproduced in mythology" (12: 381, *sic.*).

3) Nevertheless, the concept of natural religion cannot be equated with the religion of nature if the latter is defined as the deification of natural objects. For, on the one hand, according to Schelling, the deification of nature in general is out of the question because consciousness has been kept in a state of ecstasy toward nature from the start. On the other hand, in the original mythological process conscious-

ness is not concerned with natural objects themselves, but with God, who is apprehended in them, who inspires consciousness. To clarify this, Schelling distinguishes between formal and material gods (13: 188). The formal gods are the three potencies, which act as causes of the entire process, and by whose agency the material gods proceed from consciousness. Only with Egyptian mythology, the first complete mythology, do the formal gods in themselves enter consciousness, and their pure realization occurs only in the Greek mysteries. The material gods are related to the formal gods as natural products are related to the processes that produce them. The truth of mythology lies in the process and not in the product,[7] in the inner generation of the mythological representation that happens necessarily and not in the expression of it, which is free and spontaneous although it is guided by the representation. The expression of the mythological idea was always, as it were, a translation from inner vision into external presentation. But this was, in some sense, a free translation (12:-370). This explains why mythological representations are often irrational.

Schelling summarized his interpretation of the representations of the gods in the following points: I. Mythological representations are purely inward products of human consciousness. Man was aware that these representations were produced within himself by an irresistible power. II. They are not the products of a special function of consciousness, but of its substance. Consciousness was able to free itself from its entanglement with them only after a long and fearful struggle. III. They are not creations of consciousness in its essential nature, rather they are the result of an involuntary process that is external to it. IV. They become real for consciousness because their ground is the objective or theogenic principle in itself (12: 127ff.).

4) By defining mythology as natural religion, the concept

of natural religion itself has been assigned a significance that is foreign to the meaning usually given to it by rationalistic philosophies of religion. According to the latter, it signified "that religion which is the product of pure reason, of science, or of philosophy in particular; in brief, it was interpreted as rational religion" (13: 190). "For rationalism is that endeavor, conceived in free cognition or by means of reason, which desires to know about no other religion except pure rational religion, and about no other being, and therefore about no other relationship with God except that of reason related to itself" (13: 192). And, on this point, the philosophy of the Enlightenment, or subjective rationalism, and Idealism, or objective rationalism, are altogether alike (13: 192n). Both lack a principle of religion that is altogether independent of reason. Therefore, they produce no actual religion, for in the science of reason there is only religion "within the limits of pure reason" (11: 568). "The fact that one *knows* nothing of God is the result of pure rationalism, which seeks to understand everything through itself" (11: 568).

The following represents rational religion as it was construed at the conclusion of the rational process: it is contemplation that evolves in three stages: the feeling of piety, artistic intuition, and intellectual intuition.[8] It originates in opposition to the categorical imperative, and is once more overthrown by it. In this construction, Schelling has ascribed principal significance to his own development. His starting point was the Kantian-Fichtean philosophy with its emphasis on morality. In opposition to this he turned to aesthetic Idealism. Intuition in nature and in art, which was never intended without some religious connection, took the place of action. With the system of identity, intuition became intellectual in a strict sense, and it reached its goal in mystical participation in the self-intuition of absolute identity. At this high point in the development of the contemplative principle, there occurred a counterthrust. To be able to explain the world in which he must act, Schelling became an irrationalist. He recognized that mysticism cannot reach the God who acts, who as person is sought by the person; that mysticism remains bound by what is nature in God; and that on account of the Fall it has become estranged from God. Even though it transcends all the material elements of mythology and reaches the spiritual potency, it still lives within the realm of the cosmic spirit. It is basically pagan, and its ground is natural religion.[9] Whereas mythology is actual religion, although false, contemplation is unreal, ideal religion, although the false principle that gives reality to paganism has disappeared from its consciousness. It was the task of this unreal religion of reason to be a guide leading from the religion that is false though real to the religion that is both true and real, to free religion from its original bondage so that it might become religion that is truly free and spiritual. Rational religion is only a transitional phenomenon; it leads to freedom, but it is still law. The transition from rational religion to revelation is analogous to the transition from law to gospel[10] (11: 571).

4. Revealed and Philosophical Religion

1). The concept of revelation has a comprehensive significance for Schelling. It includes Judaism and Christianity within itself, and signifies the supernatural efficacy of the second potency in contrast to its natural efficacy in paganism. Therefore, it is necessary, in the first place, to clarify the antithesis of natural and supernatural for Schelling. The formation of these concepts is fundamentally determined by the idealist protest against pre-Kantian supernaturalism. This polemic is rooted in the principle of identity and finds its most vivid expression in Schelling's philosophy of nature. "The philosophy that formerly prevailed believed that it could not separate God far enough from nature; it also supposed that it was necessary to deny everything divine in nature. In fact, it produced nothing except an unnatural God on the one hand, and a godless nature on the other" (13: 188f.). Schelling expressed his own feeling of opposition to this viewpoint by saying that this "unnatural supernaturalism is indeed the same as the customary system of merely formal orthodoxy . . . it is obvious why all sincere and free spirits are opposed to it" (13: 189). Whereas the philosophy of nature was the natural antithesis of supernaturalism, the synthesis of both was given in the doctrine of nature in God and in the concept of monotheism as the doctrine of all-comprehensive unity [*All-Einheitslehre*]. The world is not natural because it is outside God—that it is outside God is not intrinsic to it, but is due to an unnatural and antidivine act—rather it is natural because the necessity of God, being that is potentiated threefold [*das dreifach potenzierte Sein*], is realized within it. But beyond being stands the lord of being; beyond necessity, the freedom of God; and beyond the potencies and their separation, the spiritual and personal unity. And each side is conditioned by the other. "God is God, that is, the supernatural, precisely on account of the nonbeing of that which he would be *mera natura,* in a purely natural way" (12: 44). The necessary correlate of the spiritual unity of God is the possibility that allows the potencies to move into tension; the correlate of God's lordship over being is the fact that what is belongs to him [*das Seiende sein Seiendes ist*]; the correlate of his freedom is the necessity by which he is free. "The supernatural itself must not be thought of as beyond all connection or relation to the natural. The supernatural is above all only there, with the natural, and it becomes known only in its victory over it, only so far as it breaks through the natural . . . therefore, supernatural religion follows only natural religion, which gives it substance"[11] (13: 187). "There, in the separation of the potencies, God [is], as it were, set outside of himself, exoterically, beyond his divinity; he [acts] as mere nature; here, on the other hand, in the unity of his potencies, he is esoteric, God in himself, God as he is, the supernatural. When, therefore, on account of the separation of the potencies, unity appears as original essence, then the true God, God in himself, the supernatural as such, appears, is revealed exactly by means of that separation" (13: 187). These statements express with complete clarity the manner in which the antithesis of natural and supernatural has been conceived: necessity, the separation of the potencies, is the natural; freedom, the spiritual unity of the potencies, is the supernatural. And God, as the supernatural, as freedom and personality and spirit, is the principle of revelation.[12]

2) Because the free, personal God is the God who reveals himself, therefore revelation is will and act, and is opposed to reason. For reason lives in the necessary, and therefore in the natural. It is not the organ of the supernatural. To be sure, it is the organ of spirit, but not of spirit that is free even from itself. "Reason can . . . only be eternal reason; it cannot become something other than itself, not even its opposite. The primary characteristic of reason is immutability, to be exactly itself. Whence comes the capacity to change into its opposite?" (14: 23). It does not lie in reason, but in that which is κρεῖττον τοῦ λόγου, free from its own necessity, in the primordial "that." But only experience stands over against it, as it stands over against everything positive and irrational. Experience is the organ of revelation. Therefore it is deceitful to speak of revelation

when what is meant is only a truth of reason that may be known even without revelation. "Therefore it is easy to see that either the concept of revelation is meaningless and should be abandoned altogether, or it is necessary to admit that the content of revelation is such that it not only would not but could not be known unless it were revealed" (14: 5). Only a free act establishes such a content. It can only be said of a God who acts that he reveals himself. Only a will can be revealed. "A will is not revealed except through its act" (14: 10). "So long as will remains will and does not pass over into act, it remains secret. But the act is its manifestation. Therefore, by means of its act the will is no longer secret" (14: 11). Since revelation is act it cannot be conceived as instruction. "Instruction can be given only about something that already is, about an already existing situation; something that is only somewhat clear is set forth more clearly" (14: 28). But revelation is an act by which God enters into a new relationship with man, not instruction about something always present.

But there is also "an obviously false notion implied from the secret of revealed religion, when it is supposed that the secret contains facts that necessarily remain secret, that is, unknown, or at least uncomprehended even after they have been revealed and made manifest" (14: 11). Revelation is not the imparting of a mystery but the working out of a will, which as will is mystery, but as act is manifest. The suprarationality of revelation lies not within the intellectual sphere, but within the moral sphere.[13] Man does not have to submit to incomprehensible formulas, rather, "he must broaden the smallness and narrowness of his thought to the greatness of the divine" (14: 12). He must find the courage to believe the "absolutely wonderful," the divine paradox; then all the anxiety of his spirit will disappear in faith in this boundlessness. Doubt is necessary so long as the possibility for greater progress exists, "for every possibility must become an actuality; therefore everything must be clear and manifest and decisive; no secret enemy must remain, even the final enemy must be overcome" (14: 14). The extreme limit to which progress and doubt could reach was the downfall of the potencies on account of the Fall; but God knows how to counter even this extreme with another extreme, by means of an act that dissolves all doubt, by which all change into something else is cut off (14: 14f.). "There must be a moment in the development of things where human knowledge, which possesses in itself an infinite drive toward progress and movement, must confess that it is not able to progress any further, where it is dumbfounded" (14: 27). It is the moment of the absolutely wonderful.[14]

3) In Schelling's concept of revelation, the rationalistic antithesis of revelation and redemption is overcome. By his personal act, God has revealed himself as personal. By the act of redemption, that is, the self-sacrifice of his natural sovereignty, he has redeemed mankind from the unfree, natural, and servile relationship to him and has become truly personal toward mankind. God has entered into a new relationship with man, one that is personal instead of natural, evangelical instead of legalistic, spiritual instead of unfree. This is the essence of Christianity. The only difficulty is that according to the concept of religion in general there must be a real, substantial relationship to God, whereas Christianity is said to be a free and personal relationship to God. There appears to be a contradiction between Christianity and the concept of religion in general. However, it is not a contradiction, it is only a relation of thesis and synthesis. The substantial relationship characteristic of the concept of religion in general presupposes that in the ideal world God is realized immediately in the unity of the poten-

cies. Therefore, the antithesis of the natural and the personal does not yet arise. But in Christianity, the spirituality of God opposes the potencies. In the former, consciousness is God-positing prior to all thinking and willing; in the latter, thinking and willing, which have come to exist outside God, are made to sacrifice themselves on account of the personal revelation of God. As a result, the unity of the potencies is restored, and consciousness is once more God-positing by means of a conscious decision. When this decision has been made, and when consciousness has sacrificed its anti-divine substantiality, it once more becomes God-positing according to its substantial being. The spirit is realized in him who can come only when selfhood has been returned entirely to being-as-ground, in him who is the Spirit in truth, the Holy Spirit.

4) The Holy Spirit comprehends all the potencies within himself. But consciousness does not become aware of this characteristic of the Spirit directly, because the Holy Spirit has come into the world in opposition to the natural spirit. Therefore, consciousness is dependent upon him as the personal Spirit in an exclusive sense. On the basis of this spiritual religion, philosophical religion evolves in which the exclusiveness of the personal relationship is overcome. Freedom, according to the positive philosophy, exists only when there is a possibility of another. Religious freedom exists only when the personal relationship comprehends both the personal and the natural. When this happens, then the personal element in freedom raises itself up on the basis of the natural element, just as the divine self raises itself up on the basis of the necessity that is within it. The natural relationship that is now attained is not to be construed as the false pagan relationship, but rather as the true relationship of consciousness to nature and culture in their ideality. This relationship was reached at the end of the

rational process and found its theoretical expression in a philosophy of nature that discerned the potencies of divine nature in the natural process, and also in the philosophy of spirit, which perceived the course of the entire cultural process as leading to the religion of Spirit. Philosophical religion has made rational religion subordinate to itself. Nevertheless, it too is actual religion and necessarily includes within itself the factors that belong to every actual religion. The only difference is that the principles that remain uncomprehended in all the others are grasped and understood in it (11: 250). Therefore it is only realized at the third stage [of the development of religion]. Only when both religions [revelational and philosophical] are mutually free from each other does philosophical religion, which comprehends both, become possible. And it becomes actual only when the truth of false religion is united with true religion on the ground of true religion, that is, only when nature and culture receive a religious evaluation that is based upon Christianity.[15]

II. The Concept of History

1. Time and Eternity

1) Every philosophy of history that asserts the real entry of God into history must investigate the relationship of time and eternity. In Schelling's case this was all the more important because, on account of the Kantian solution of the problem of time, a real historical mode of divine action within history had become immediately problematical, and because during the first period of his development, Schelling had not gone beyond the Kantian theory, although his formulation of it was different. "Time is the negation of

particular life in its particularity, for [the particular] arises only in time, it does not exist in itself." "For its origin and its being are only a continual passing that come to naught on account of the infinite concept of the All." "In the temporal being of things the All discerns only its own infinite life; therefore time is nothing but the All appearing in opposition to the life of particular things" (6: 220). Time is the form of the nothingness of things as individuals. "Everything is temporal whose actuality surpasses essence, or whose essence contains more than it can grasp in its actuality" (2: 364).

However, the essence of finite things, which surpasses their actuality is their idea. The notion of progress is joined to the doctrine of ideas also at this point. In the idea, the antithesis of the one and the many, and of time and timelessness, is dissolved. Neither the abstract and timeless unity of the concept nor the external, temporal manifold is characteristic of the idea. This applies in an absolute sense to the eternal, all comprehending idea, the eternal identity of all ideas. "True eternity is not eternity in contrast to time, but eternity that grasps time itself and posits it within itself as eternity. . . . It is not being in contrast to becoming, but being in eternal unity with eternal becoming" (7: 239). Traces of this formulation of the doctrine of ideas reappear throughout Schelling's later thought: "God, absolutely considered, is neither eternity nor time, but the absolute identity of eternity and time. Everything that exists in time exists eternally in him as subject, and everything that exists eternally in him as subject exists temporally in him as object" (7: 430). "True eternity is not that which entirely excludes time, but that which contains time (eternal time) subjected to itself. True eternity is the overcoming of time" (8: 260).

2) The antithesis of time and timelessness (eternity in a

strict sense) is therefore included in eternity, and this antithesis is equivalent to the idea that comprehends both:
finitude and infinity, ideality and reality, object and subject
(later, subject and object).[XXXI] But according to the law of
identity, the antithesis is not absolute. Within time, the
identity of time and eternity is subject to the power [*Exponent*] of time, and in eternity the same identity is subject to
the power of eternity. Every idea has its own, qualitative
time: "There is no external, universal time; all time is
... something intrinsic that everything has within itself, not
outside itself." Abstract time originates only through comparison of the times of different things. "The reality of time
is merely the different modifications that a being undergoes" (7: 431). The quality of a thing is the same as its
modifications, that is, its higher or lower grades of indifference.

The importance of the concept of qualitative time in-
creases when it is founded upon the irrationalism [of Schelling's later development], inasmuch as here it enters into
a real antithesis, and therefore a real distinction of times
must be conceived according to their respective qualities.
But whereas, from the standpoint of the doctrine of identity, different times exist simultaneously in the totality of
the universe—or, rather, they are nonexistent in the face of
the absolute—from the standpoint of Schelling's doctrine
of freedom, they attain a real autonomy over against identity and, therefore, against each other. From this standpoint also, they establish an organism of transcendental
(ideal), qualitative times that correspond to the three comprehensive ideas that have become potencies. Potentiality,
necessity, and goal are related to each other as past, present, and future. This explains the origin of the concept of
different times. They are different, nevertheless, they are
contemporaneous, indeed, their essence requires that they

be contemporaneous. "Past time is not anulled time [*auf-gehobene Zeit*]; certainly the past cannot exist as the present, but it must be contemporaneous as a past with its present . . . (and the same applies to the future). . ., and it is equally absurd to suppose that the being of the past as well as the being of the future is entirely nonexistent" (8: 302). Only by reference to this concept can God's eternity be united with his entry into time and with a process that is full of contradictions. "In each of his forms, as Yes or No, and as the unity of both, [God] can exist and work. But in the decisive contradiction between Yes and No he can only be conceived by means of the concept of different times" (7: 303)

3) Concretely considered, the following times are to be distinguished: "The pretemporal eternity that, on account of the creation, is posited as past time; the time of the creation itself, which is the present; the time that everything will reach through the creation, and which is related to everything as the future eternity" (4: 109). All three, however, are contained in absolute eternity, which implies nothing more than that God is, as *actus purissimus.* "For eternity must be conceived not as the collectivity of those moments of time, but as so coexisting with every particular time that in each one eternity perceives only itself (the wholly immeasurable one)" (8: 307). Eternity means that in every moment and in each of his forms God is wholly present to himself. Therefore it is no contradiction to suppose that different times exist in eternity.

In the pretemporal eternity, coming forth from the eternity that he is, God, the first potency represents himself as the possibility of a future act, and therefore as the cause of his truly divine self-consciousness. The present age begins when the pretemporal eternity is posited as the past. "There can be no time so long as there is no past. The only possible way to posit a beginning of time . . . is for something that before was not time to be posited as time, namely the past. Only a dynamic beginning of time like this one can be thought. A mechanical beginning is unthinkable" (14: 109) The present age was supposed to reach the stage of the future eternity, but it was prevented from reaching it on account of the Fall. This gives rise to the present retarded time, "which posits only itself again and again, with no true result that the third age can penetrate." "This apparent time that possesses neither a genuine past nor a genuine future is not true time . . . but only a sequence of times" (14: 109f.) This time has, in fact, been posited by man, and it is to it that the Kantian critique applies. It is the form of nothingness of particular things that are estranged from the idea.[16] Present time is related to the second age as the ages are related to absolute eternity. "The original being of man must be conceived of . . . only as supratemporal being and as the essential eternity that, in contrast to time, is itself only a timeless moment" (11: 141). Just as eternity coexists with every age, so man's supratemporal act of self-position coexists with every temporal act. The supratemporal act is realized in the temporal. Here, cause and effect form no temporal sequence, but are related as supratemporal act (called in less precise terms, pretemporal act) and intratemporal realization.[17] And just as eternity unfolds itself in an organism of qualitative times, so also does the supratemporal act become explicit in the present time.

2. Philosophy of History and Historical Philosophy

1) The contrast between Hegel and Schelling can be grasped in the formula "philosophy of history and historical philosophy." However, the contrast is not absolute. On the one hand, Hegel had included in his philosophy of

history elements that belong to historical philosophy—in Schelling's judgment this was clearly unjustifiable; on the other one hand, the philosophy of history forms an important part of Schelling's entire system. And what is more, Hegel led the way in this line of thought, both formally and materially. In his *Lectures on the Method of Academic Study,* in the important eighth lecture, Schelling defined theology as "the highest synthesis of philosophical and historical knowledge" (5: 286). In Christianity the universe is viewed as history and "therefore Christianity is in its inmost spirit and in its highest meaning historical" (5: 288). "But that synthesis with history, without which theology would be inconceivable, requires in return as its condition the Christian view of history" (5: 291). From the Christian viewpoint, the ancient world is the part of history that corresponds to nature. "The culmination of ancient time and the beginning of modern time, whose ruling principle was the infinite, could only be achieved when what is truly infinite entered the finite, not in order to deify it, but in order to sacrifice it in its own person to God and, thereby, to reconcile it. The primary idea of Christianity is God who has become incarnate in man. Christ is the culmination and the end of the ancient world of the gods" (5: 292). The Incarnation represents the specific demand of any construction of the philosophy of history as well as its starting point. It is noteworthy that already here, as it was later in full measure in the work of Hegel, the principles of the construction are religious: The self-revelation of God in his two comprehending ideas provides the scheme of the construction. "On account of [the] universality of its idea, the historical construction of Christianity is inconceivable apart from the religious construction of history as a whole" (5: 299). And this religious construction forms the essence, the characteristic content of history. History is the unfolding of the

ideas that are contained in identity under the power of the
infinite. The eternal alternates between the finite and the
infinite, between nature and history. But just as nature
contains gravity and light, each in their turn, so there is
within history a nature period and a history period. The
entire construction is founded upon the doctrine of ideas,
and shares the limitations of that standpoint, namely, the
negative evaluation of everything temporal in contrast to
eternity. At the central point there is a breakthrough:
"Theologians interpret the incarnation of God in Christ
. . . empirically, namely, at a specific moment in time God
assumed human nature. But thought can make absolutely
nothing of this, for God is eternally beyond all time. The
incarnation of God is therefore the incarnation of eternity.
Christ, the man, in his manifestation, is only the culmination [of history] because he is also as well its beginning" (5:
297f.) History is the history of the ideas, but the eternal
stands beyond every idea. Schelling's doctrine of freedom
marks the transition to historical philosophy. Because God
is a life, and not merely a being, he has subjected himself
to passion and becoming. "Without the concept of a human
suffering God, which is common to all the mysteries and
spiritual religions, history as a whole remains incomprehensible" (7: 403). God enters history, but he is bound to
the historical process. He does not posit it or stand over
against it in freedom. The relationship between God's eternity and his temporal existence has not [yet] been made
clear. [The interpretation of it] lies midway between
philosophy of history and historical philosophy. It is implicit in Schelling's doctrine of freedom and fully developed in Hegel's system.

2) The irrational principle rooted in the philosophy of
nature led Schelling on to a completely historical philosophy, that is, to a positive philosophy.[18] Historical philoso-

phy is a more appropriate and expressive name for positive philosophy. "The God of a truly historical or positive philosophy does not follow a natural course, he acts." (13: 125). He needs no logical process to attain perfection. He is not the end but the beginning. "To rationalism, nothing can originate from a deed, for example, from a free and spontaneous creation. It recognizes only essential relationships. Everything happens merely *modo aeterno,* in an eternal, that is, purely logical, manner by means of an immanent movement" (3: 124). Historical philosophy is the domain of freedom, will, and act, which, in the final analysis, is religion. The subject of historical philosophy is divine history whose nucleus is the history of religion. Its task is to interpret actual religion. It is concerned with the great acts of freedom that found the divine-human relationship, namely, creation, fall, and redemption. It treats the latter in a three-fold sense: extrinsic redemption in paganism, mediated redemption in Judaism, intrinsic, unmediated redemption in Christianity. The protest against the rationalistic view of history receives a new clarity and emphasis: "The historical itself . . . is the essential characteristic of Christianity." The historical is not something incidental to doctrine, but is doctrine itself. It would be a poor interpretation that construed doctrine as essence or substance and the historical as form or clothing. Of course, what is at issue is not the "universal-historical", but a "higher historical," "history that involves the divine itself, a divine history" (13: 195). Historical philosophy is concerned with history that is rooted in the supra-historical. Empirical history is its object only so far as supra-historical history realizes its purpose within it.

3) Thus, the philosophy of history is assigned a place within the framework of historical philosophy. In his account of rational philosophy, that is, in his account of the

"rational process" given above, Schelling included a construction of history. But the rational process came to an end with the advent of Christianity, whereby rational philosophy as well as philosophy of history was assigned to the pre-Christian period of history. But the construction of Church history in Schelling's *Exposition of the Philosophy of Pure Reason* also contains outlines of a—post-Christian—philosophy of history. Therefore, the relationship of philosophy of history and historical philosophy must be defined as follows: the philosophy of history receives its framework from historical philosophy. It falls into two parts, separated by the fact of revelation which has a suprahistorical basis. The parts are not continuous. Each part has its own beginning and end. The construction of the pre-Christian rational process begins with prehistorical time, which is characterized by a complete absence of culture. It demonstrates the progressive rise of culture until it reaches perfection and catastrophe in Hellenism. The philosophy of post-Christian history likewise begins with a condition of cultural bondage. It treats the growing autonomy of cultural life and points to its goal, that is, the development of the unity of religion and culture in philosophical religion. Whereas on the ground of paganism, religion and culture diverged until they reached their ultimate separation with the advent of revelation, in the history of Christianity they develop a tendency to converge. The unity is the principle of an immanent eschatology.[19] (Beyond this and beside this, transcendent eschatology preserves its independent validity.)

4) Although Schelling set philosophical religion as the goal of the historical process, the principle of irrationalism on which historical philosophy was founded led him to conclude that this goal could never be regarded as fully realized. Since historical philosophy is nothing but the con-

stantly growing proof of the actually existing God, and since "the realm of actuality in which God moves is neither perfected nor concluded, but is constantly approaching perfection, therefore the proof [of God's existence] is never completed, and this science is only *philo-sophia*"[20](13: 131). "Even the present is not a boundary, even here a view opens up into a future that is nothing but the continuing proof . . . of what is no longer merely that which is . . . but what transcends that which is [*das Überseiende*]" (13: 132). To be sure, the future possibilities are not related to something that passes beyond the basic acts of the Fall or of revelation; rather they are related to developments that do not forsake the soil of revelational religion, for in revelation supra-historical history reaches its decisive crisis.

3. Supra-Historical and Empirical History

1) Schelling applies the concept of the supra-historical in the first place to the fact of the Fall. It is "the original fact itself (the beginning of history), the fact, the event κατ' ἐξοχην." "This event—as well as all that led up to it— occurs entirely within the supra-historical." "It is the supra-historical beginning of mythology . . ." (12: 153). The Fall is supra-historical inasmuch as it stands beyond actual history. However, at the same time it is the condition of history, indeed, as the realization of the Fall, history to a degree includes it within itself. But the concept of the supra-historical means more than this. In the second quotation given in this section, it is stated that everything that leads up to the Fall is to be construed together with it as supra-historical. This leads to the conclusion that even in the supra-historical a time sequence and, therefore, a history are presupposed. The time sequence in question here is the organism of qualitative times, and the history is di-

vine history, which runs its course according to this sequence of times. The concept of the supra-historical applies especially to this characteristic of history to be divine
history, and it also applies to those divine acts that are the
causes of special phenomena within actual history.[21] Schelling then equates the transcendent with the supra-historical
and sets it in contrast to empirical history. "History appears
to be deprived of all divine content whenever it is deprived
of its connection with that inner, divine, transcendent history that literally is the only true history, history κατ᾽ ἐξ
οχήν" (14: 220). *"Whoever is ignorant of supra-historical history
has nowhere to put a personality such as Christ"* (14: 35). "To be
sure, Christ in his historical manifestation is the immediate
object of interpretation. But precisely this historical manifestation can only be explained in a context that extends
beyond it, on the one hand, back to the beginning of things,
and on the other, to the final end of things. Nevertheless,
the content of Christianity is not so-called universal religion. Its content is the particular personality, who, ever
since the beginning of the present order of things outside
God, although he was an autonomous personality, did not
cling to his existence as a personality, but only used it by
willingly subjecting himself and offering himself up in order to transform the divine disfavor once more into a mer-
ciful goodwill" (14: 228). Supra-historical history is
trinitarian history.[22]

2) The polemic against Schelling's positive philosophy,
which compares it with mythology, gnosticism, or theosophy, is directed primarily against the concept of trinitarian
history. For the sake of historical clarity, it is necessary at
this point to inquire into this concept. The first difficulty
with respect to the doctrine of the trinity is that Schelling
conceived of the reality of the trinitarian relationship in a
historical development. The age of the Father is the state

of the purely potential trinity; there is as yet no three-fold act of will in which God comprehends himself.[23] The age of the Son, which begins with the creation, is the state of real separation, of tension within the trinity. In the age of the Spirit, there is a conscious, willed unity. But, for the eternal God, the separation of these three ages is not such that they could not be altogether present to him as "different times." They are ideal times, that is, times in which the identity of the one and the many stands under the predominance of unity. Elevation through opposition is nothing but the expression of the vitality and the reality of the personal trinitarian life of God, as well as the presupposition of his entry into real time.

This gives rise to difficulties concerning the concept of theogony. Schelling applied the term primarily to the mythological process, but he also applied it to the processes of nature and of revelation. It should be clear that the concept does not have the same sense of pagan theogonies or cosmogonies. In general, it does not signify the supra-worldly personal life of God; rather, it signifies the potencies that epistemology and the metaphysical doctrine of principles have found to be the ultimate facts of all cosmic events. The connection between the potencies and the trinitarian life of god results only through the fundamental notion of the relationship of God and world, and this notion ultimately concerns every opinion and judgment of historical philosophy: God is related to the world in the same way as his personal self is related to his nature. But as personality God is not bound by his nature. These two statements comprise Schelling's doctrine of God. His doctrine of the trinity is only an application of the general notion of the relation of God and world to the special trinitarian relationship. Whoever would dispute this application must first of all clarify his position concerning its presupposition.[24]

Once the construction of the concept of God is accepted in principle, it remains to inquire into its structure in detail. Concerning the first potency, not only is the ambiguity of its determinations free of difficulties, but it is perfectly suited to explain all the others. The statement that the first potency, as the principle of divine wrath, has the right to destroy the creature, and that God himself cannot deprive it of this right on account of his holiness, sounds more mythological than philosophical. But this mode of expression becomes understandable as soon as it is recalled that the will of the first potency is the will of infinite subjectivity, which has been aroused by man, and that his will, which represents the one unitary act, can only be overcome on the most profound level, where it has become absolutely effective. Every conquest of the will-to-selfhood by the repressive restraint of an external agent (every arbitrary mitigation of the wrath of God) would be unethical. Even God can overcome the will only through the will itself, if he would not destroy it. Since the will of the wrath of God and the will of sin are one and the same, Schelling's doctrine of reconciliation is not mythological, but ethical.

For his treatment of the third potency, Schelling correctly refers to the Johannine testimony of the coming of the Spirit after the glorification of the Son. His doctrine of the Spirit—as well as his clear distinction between cosmic and divine spirit—possesses the realism of the biblical doctrine. The unity of the universal and the individual in the trinitarian personalities could give all three potencies a mythological character. But their unity is rooted in the doctrine of ideas. In the idea, the antithesis of abstract universal and concrete individual is overcome. The essence of the idea is the unity of both. And the absolute idea is the identity of the absolute universal and the absolute individual. These are three all-comprehensive ideas with one determination. Schelling has strongly emphasized that his principles are not abstractions, that despite their universal validity they are thoroughly concrete. To him, the most serious reproach against a philosophy is that it moves in abstractions. The potencies are neither universal concepts of reflection, nor mythological individuals.[25] The second potency is an exception to the preceding arguments, for assertions are made about it whose mythological character cannot be denied. This is primarily the case with statements about the incarnation of the second potency. But this requires a special inquiry.

4. Inner and Outer History

1) Schelling himself was aware of the difficulties within his system caused by the deduction of the Incarnation as an external, empirical fact. For this reason, he tried to find a historical solution to the problem. I quote at length: "Let us imagine a person who has received a strictly rationalistic education, who has no prior knowledge of Christianity, and who is suddenly confronted by it. Inevitably he will feel compelled to explain its appearance exactly as he must have felt, in a similar situation, the necessity to explain mythology. For the latter will hardly seem more strange to him than the former. But now the important distinction between the two becomes apparent. There is nothing historical in mythological representations except that at a certain time they were believed by a certain race. . . . But we find no reason to ascribe historical truth to the persons who are objects of these representations" (14: 229). "But Christ is not a mere phenomenon; he lived as another man, was born, and died, and his historical existence is verified as much as the existence of any other historical person" (14: 230). "If it were possible to doubt the historical truth of his

person, then one might be tempted to represent Christianity as a continuation, or strictly speaking, as the necessary end of the mythological process" (14: 230). In this case, Christianity might be interpreted as follows: through suffering and death the second potency necessarily became a past event for human consciousness, thereby the third potency came near and made a complete end to paganism. This interpretation might have applied "had it not been made entirely impossible by the unique fact that Christ was a historical personality who did not merely make an appearance, but who lived and suffered before the eyes of the world like any other man" (14: 230f.). But even though the historical reality of the person of Christ is indisputable, the mythological interpretation of the Gospel history, which attributed all the divine qualities ascribed to Jesus to a mythical glorification, might still be brought into question. However, to explain how this glorification came about, the majesty of Christ must be presupposed. The Gospel histories are not necessary to account for the exaltation of Christ, "on the contrary, the exaltation of Christ, with all the meaning that we attach to it, is necessary to comprehend the Gospel" (14: 233). Moreover, Strauss's mythical interpretation is founded on a "schoolboyish" application of Hegelian concepts, whose truth is presupposed as if it were incontestable. But "the question of the significance and the reality of revelation depends upon a crisis of philosophy itself, which must have and has actually taken place" (14: 231). Therefore, the question reverts again to the systematic sphere, and must be decided there.

2) In the entire construction of the history of religion, two lines of thought can be distinguished, which are related as ground and consequence; the supra-historical trinitarian history and the inner history of human consciousness. Accordingly, the question of necessity of an empirical incarna-

tion falls into two parts: I. Is the empirical, external incarnation of the second potency necessary for the completion of supra-historical history? II. Is it necessary for the completion of the inner history of consciousness? Concerning the first question, it must be pointed out first of all that Schelling conceived of the self-abasement of the logos as a unitary act that began with the beginning of the mythological process, and that turned the entire pre-Christian history into a history of the suffering of the second potency. "The passion of the Messiah does not begin . . . with his incarnation. The Messiah suffers from the beginning, he has been set in a condition of negative suffering ever since he was restored to human consciousness . . . as pure potency" (12: 317). Because his dominion in human consciousness is the seat of his divine majesty, the forfeiture of this dominion is the passion of the Son. He does not need to become man to suffer. All the less in order to be tempted, for the real temptation occurs in his pre-existence[26] (14: 169). Thus it remains to inquire about his death. However, his death, as far as it is applicable only to the supra-historical sphere, is the absolute renunciation by the logos of his realization within consciousness and outside God. Whereas his passion in paganism is his struggle for actualization, his death is his voluntary and complete abandonment of it after he has fought for it. In this way, the argument is clear and consistent in itself. An external, factual incarnation can in no way be deduced from this.

The answer to the second question must be no less negative. In the whole of paganism, God is discerned in the products of nature, which correspond to the stages of the mythological process of nature. But that God is perceived in them does not in any way imply his identity to them. Rather, it implies that the God who rules human consciousness provides it with an intuition of itself, which is located

within the individual finite natural object, but which goes
beyond its particular content to the idea. In Christianity,
God comes to consciousness personally, spiritually, and
historically. Here he can be perceived only in a historical
personality. However, to be historical means to sacrifice
oneself in one's naturalness in order to find oneself in one's
spirituality. This intuition was given in Christ, and therefore in him God has become personal to man. In this life
and death of him who conceived of himself as the son of
man and the lord of mankind, and who sacrificed himself
for mankind, the logos created an intuition of the estranged
being of every natural spirit that is not free from itself and
cannot sacrifice itself. And as he created this intuition, the
logos sacrificed himself in his natural dominion over consciousness and caused the coming of the Holy Spirit. The
necessity of the actual Incarnation is also not established on
this ground.[27]

Although the doctrine of the empirical incarnation of the
second potency is untenable in Schelling's philosophy
when considered systematically, it is nevertheless very clear
indeed how he came to it. Here too, Schelling's starting
point was the opinion of the rationalists that the historical
element of Christianity was an inadequate clothing for eternal truths of reason. His very early protest against this
conception led Schelling to the viewpoint of his *Lectures on
the Methods of Academic Study:* In Christianity the idea is discerned in historical phenomena, so that through a historical personality paganism has become the past. Finally, the
historicity of Christianity is to be looked for not only in the
fact that the idea is discerned in history, but that it has
actually entered history. A supra-historical history is the
basis of the internal history of consciousness. The three
stages of Schelling's development on his way to the conception of "historical philosophy" are the nonhistorical [ra-

tional], internal history, and supra-historical history. The nearer the goal, the stronger is his polemic against the rationalistic starting point, and the more energetic his will to maintain the historical in its full right. This interest that is both polemical and positive led Schelling back beyond the rationalist critique of the externally historical, which was the startingpoint of the whole development, and thereby caused him to incorporate a heterogeneous element [in his system]. However, once the historical element of Christianity is viewed in its purely external actuality, the fundamental position of Idealism has been abandoned. Then, external history can have meaning only by providing an intuition of internal history. Therefore it is clearly necessary that a man should come who offers the intuition of the self-sacrificing and justifying God, a man who, by coming, makes this sacrifice objectively possible in the supra-historical sphere. Without the external fact, revelation could not have happened. However, the content of revelation is not the external fact, but the supra-historical fact. This critique of Schelling, derived from his system, is also his defense against the accusation that he created a new mythology.

NOTES

Part I

1. The interpretation of Kant suggested here and in what follows should not be taken as the author's. Rather it is meant to indicate the emergence of Schelling's thought from Kant as Schelling himself represented it. Moreover, the truth of Schelling's position does not depend upon the validity of his interpretation of Kant. The same applies to Schelling's estimate of the remaining philosophical standpoints mentioned here. Wherever the author draws parallels independently with other philosophers, these are either put in the notes or designated expressly as such.

2. However, practically it is correct. Whereas Fichte posited the nonego in opposition to the ego for a practical purpose only, and gave only a teleological interpretation to the latter, [Schelling] separated the philosophy of nature from ethics only to reunite them again in his philosophy of religion. However, this reunion was only temporary, for the final implications of the philosophy of nature are worked out only in his historical philosophy. Whereas for Fichte action proceeds from the ego only, for Schelling, the ego in itself is the product of a dual action.

3. The material concept of freedom finds its perfect expression in Schelling's concept of identity. Whereas in Spinoza's system the identity of freedom and necessity (freedom = absolute self-determination) stand under the predominance of necessity, and in Fichte's system, under the predominance of freedom, with Schelling their identity is perfectly realized. The construction of this principle was the negative presupposition for the inclusion of a formal (irrational) movement into the concept of freedom.

4. If Eduard von Hartmann believes that he has found in Schelling a predeces-

sor in the construction of this concept, it is because he has read into Schelling's thought Schopenhauer's concept of the will, which clearly excludes ideas, and because he has failed to see that in the concept of potency the Spinozistic antithesis of thought and extension has been overcome. In short, he forgets that for Schelling identity has a cognitive and theoretical character that struggles against separation and follows pre-critical paths.

5. In this way, Schelling came to regard Plato as the forerunner of the Christian view of reality. This is clear at two points: [Schelling's] concept of intuition includes a two-fold protest against the Enlightenment, namely, against the intellectualism of abstract reflection and the moralism of an abstract ethic. Hence, his intense struggle against reflective understanding and the categorical imperative. But this conflict called forth two other no less questionable phenomena: mysticism and quietism. The more intellectual intuition became, the less it was able to affirm individual phenomena as such, and the more it became necessary to find some other way to evaluate them. The result was that after his Platonic period, Schelling restricted intellectual intuition to the ideas, whereas in the phenomenal world understanding and law came to prevail in their own right. However, since his estimate of them remained fundamentally the same, the phenomenal world now appeared to be a deviation from the norm. As in his earlier period, the world of ideas was still the norm. A comparison with Schleiermacher testifies to the importance of Platonism for Schelling. In his protest against the Enlightenment and in his concept of intuition, Schleiermacher took the same starting point as Schelling. Nevertheless, besides intuition as objective consciousness, he also emphasized feeling as nonobjective or passive consciousness. As he came closer to Schelling's system of identity, feeling increased in importance proportionally as intuition became more abstract, speculative, and without an object. Schleiermacher followed Schelling no further, i.e., beyond Platonism to the theory of freedom, therefore he remained in many ways farther away from the Christian tradition.

6. This definition of the formal concept of freedom depends upon the material concept. Since freedom as self-position does not signify something absolutely lifeless, pure being, but means rather "to posit oneself as self-positing," then it must include a "potency" for self-contradiction. That it can posit itself *as* itself presupposes an antithesis that has been overcome. Since we are concerned with the absolute, we can only speak here of an irrational self-contradiction in the absolute.

7. Cf. Hegel, *Religionsphilosophie*, 2d ed., 1: 202: "The spiritual is the absolute unity of the spiritual and the natural, such that the latter is only something posited or contained by the spirit." "The highest determination of spirit is self-consciousness, which produces this objectivity within itself" (p. 66): "The other that is known by the absolute spirit is the spirit itself. Only that is absolute spirit which knows itself" (p. 200). For Hegel, spirit is self-cognition: it posits another in order to become self-conscious. For Schelling, spirit is self-willing: it posits its contradiction in order to choose itself in freedom. In Hegel's system nature and spirit

are related as negation and position. In Schelling's system will and anti-will are related as position and counterposition. Hegel only interprets the other teleologically (so that it may be conceived as spirit). Schelling gives an aetiological explanation as well (because there is an irrational moment in the will).

8. How much this turnabout owes to the influence of Boehme and Baader requires a special inquiry. In any case, Schelling was not diverted by them from his course of development that started from Kant, as a glance at Kant's doctrine of radical evil will prove, for in this doctrine lies the seed of the irrationalism of Schelling's second major period. In my opinion, Baader's influence is completely analogous to the influence of Plato or Spinoza. In every case, critical philosophy remained the basis upon which older philosophical formulations were received, so that the critical foundation of Schelling's philosophy remained unshaken. However, the structure of Schelling's thought was modified according as a new turn was prepared for by the working out of its idealistic thesis and as congenial elements of other systems gained an influence over the new formulation. According to this conception [of Schelling's development], the strong formal influence of Baader and Boehme on Schelling's *On the Nature of Human Freedom,* among other works, could not lead him off his course.

9. The first potency is the principle of subjectivity, inasmuch as by means of the elevation of the irrational will the unity within identity is destroyed and everything attains selfhood whose basis is the irrational ground of all creatures; i.e., the first potency is subject (ὑποκείμενον) inasmuch as it is the ground of every egoistic *(selbstischer)* individual or will. The culmination of subjectivity occurs in the human ego, or, as Schelling called it against Fichte, in the principle of original sin. In Fichte's subjective idealism it became a universal principle, so that it might remain the basis. This reversal of the meaning of the concepts subject and object follows the meaning of the words themselves and scholastic usage: objective-ideal, subjective-real.

10. Schelling's significance for the history of philosophy can be seen perfectly in this concept, which is the *crux philosophiae* from Parmenides to Hegel. He has defined the ambiguous character of that which is not positively and concretely by means of the irrational will. It is the principle of the freedom of God and man; it is the nothingness from which the world has been created; and it is what ought not to be, which is the power of sin and error. Schelling's interpretation of the first potency is an ontology of nonbeing.

11. This doctrine of the potencies is clarified as well as evaluated by a historical arrangement of philosophical tendencies according to their attitudes toward the potencies: A one-sided emphasis on the second potency, on necessity (the necessity of reason, eternal, purely logical truths) as it was advocated by the Leibniz-Wolffian school has been made impossible by Kant's critique of rationalism. (Nevertheless, it was revived in the work of Krause.) A strong emphasis on the third and an insufficient consideration of the first potency is characteristic of Fichte and Hegel. Both dwell on the ought to be; their interpretation of the world is teleological. They comprise the idealistic wing of Idealism. Eduard von Hart-

mann combines the first and the second potencies. But because in his system the will lacks the idea and the idea lacks will, he is not able to reach the third potency, and the world process ends for him as for Schopenhauer in nothingness. Finally, Nietzsche combines the first and the third potencies. The second, universal potency, is entirely lacking in his system. Emphasis on the third potency leads to an evolutionary optimism; emphasis on the first potency, to pessimism. Rational optimism toward the present is, along with the second potency, pushed into the background.

12. With certain modifications, this concept of God has been operative in Schleiermacher's *Glaubenslehre*.

13. Otherwise his aseity would be confined to this point. Therefore, we may distinguish Schelling's doctrine of nature in God from his earlier doctrine. Earlier, as the creator of the idealist philosophy of nature, he had maintained that nature is not something objective or material, in the pre-critical sense, but rather is will and act. On this basis, representations of God, for example, of his corporeality, can above all be avoided.

14. The point of view of *On the Nature of Human Freedom* has had an influence on theology by way of Hegel (looking back toward the standpoint of Schelling's *Lectures on the Method of Academic Study* and his *System of Transcendental Idealism*) and by way of the speculative theology dependent upon him, on the one hand, through the theistic systems of the younger Fichte and Weisse and, on the other, through the theology of mediation, which takes a similar position. It is also possible to demonstrate its effect upon theosophically· influenced realism (demonology, eschatology).

15. Schelling himself perceived this, as is demonstrated by the fact that the work on which the foregoing discussion is based, *The Ages of the World*, was announced repeatedly by him yet was never published, so that it remained an unpublished fragment (cf. 8: 195). First of all, it is evident that nature in God, which originally corresponded to the first potency, now embodies the three potencies. As was pointed out above, this agrees with the change in the concept of potency. If, in the concept of potency, the possibility exists of becoming unequal to oneself, then the concept of potency applies to the second and third potencies as well, inasmuch as identity can only be unequal to itself, because in the first potency it possesses the power to restore unity, and in the third, the power that leads toward the goal. The world process is the actualizing of the three potencies through the elevation of the first. So long as God was conceived as evolving through the world process, the triad of potencies was sufficient to describe the concept of God. But once the spirituality of God was conceived apart from the world process and spirituality was represented as an eternal process, the concept of potency could no longer apply to the stages of this process because it had now become an eternal actuality. On the other hand, if God has the power to depart from himself, then the creative potency is preserved. The result is a duplication of principles: the ideal in God forms together with his nature his eternal spirituality; nature included the potencies within itself to form a world outside of God. The great

difficulties in this account, which derive from the double meaning of nature in God, are overcome only in the positive philosophy. The notion of the ideal principle, of the divine self, is important and of significance for all that follows. Whereas nature is the embodiment of the potencies, the ideal is nonpotent, it is "tranquil bliss that is completely self-fulfilled and thinks of nothing, like a quiet inwardness that agrees with itself and is not aware of its own nonbeing" (8: 236). Whereas nature is the identity of unity and multiplicity under the power of multiplicity, the ideal is identity under the power of unity and therefore without potency.

16. In this sense, Schelling's usage identifies theism with deism. Both words signify a unitarian denial of the universality of God and therefore of all positive doctrines that transcend the mere positing of the concept of God (12: 77). The modern "concept of theism" derives essentially from the theistic philosophy beginning with *On the Nature of Human Freedom*, and corresponds more closely to Schelling's *Monotheism* [*Philosophie der Mythologie: Erstes Buch*].

17. In this entire construction Dorner overlooks the definition of God as an absolutely moral being (cf. I. A. Dorner, *Gesammelte Schriften*, [Berlin, 1883]). But as in Schelling's system generally, so also in his concept of God, ethical content is not to be found in a particular part but throughout the entire construction (cf. the editor's [K. F. A. Schelling's] foreword, 12:xi, *sic.*). The moral element in Schelling's thought derives from the voluntaristic character of his entire system, and specifically from the definitions of the relationship of the potencies to each other, of their harmony and their indissolubility even when in tension. The good is the agreement of God with himself. But if the good in general is to be equated with God, then it is necessary that compelling reasons for this identification exist in the construction of the concept of God itself. It is not enough simply to transfer the idea of the good to the concept of God unless one can show what this transfer means for the concept of God. Hence, the alternative between power and love as the highest designation of God is not considered by Schelling. Indeed, according to him, God's divinity lies in his lordship over all being. He does not recognize any other concept of God. However, lordship is nothing but an expression of the perfect freedom and spirituality of God. And in this sense, even Dorner's definition of love as the unity of self-affirmation and self-denial can be applied to Schelling's concept of God. The spiritual unity of God remains indissoluable even in the separation of the potencies. God can give himself up to the world because he remains lord of the world and because he affirms himself in it and through it. God is good, for he is perfect spirit. Cf. [J. Chr. K.] Hofmann, *Schriftbeweis*, Lehrgang 1: 5: "For this reason, because he is triune, God chooses to become the man of God. His will is coeternal with his triune nature, and his triunity is the same as his love." Here also there is a complete unity of the formal and material aspects of the concept of God, for without both aspects the form of certainty would be lacking. We know God as the perfect spirit because we know him as the good.

18. The arguments that Schelling provides here are well suited to overcome

the common misunderstanding of aprioristic philosophy, when it claims to deduce facts a priori and hence to prove their existence. This is made possible by the clear recognition of the difference between essence and existence. This evaluation of Hegel, which here is free of malice, in fact touches a sore point in his system, namely, the transition from logic to the philosophy of nature. Schelling demanded that Hegel limit himself to a phenomenology of spirit and not presume to interpret the world as it actually exists.

19. We have shown above how moral and intellectual motives led Schelling to take up the doctrine of ideas and thereby to overcome the original (aesthetic) doctrine of the immediate intuition of the infinite in the finite. Here the aesthetic doctrine of irony itself leads the way: intuition cannot stop with the finite individual. Every individual is posited in order to be annulled. The truth of the finite is only to be interpreted ironically. Absolute truth alone is the ironist, namely, God, who allows himself to be seen in the finite. In this way, Fichte scored a victory over aesthetic idealism in its original form.

20. The presupposition of this entire train of thought is Kant's demonstration of the contradictions that arise when the concepts of reflection are applied to the transcendent realm. Freedom and spirit are inconceivable to the understanding because they are transcendent. The spirit is the absolutely miraculous [*Wunder*], to use Hegel's expression. The dialectical method is not an "invasion of Romanticism" into Kant's idealism, rather it is a consistent extension of it.

21. This statement is as well a characteristic formulation of Schelling's pessimism, which applied to the original process of nature and consequently to the development of the world of ideas, and not just to the world after the Fall.

22. Schelling did not develop this idea in a trinitarian context. However, the trinitarian construction is doubtless fundamental to it.

23. It must not be forgotten here that we are describing the original process of nature, i.e., the evolution of the world of ideas, which is from the present standpoint supra-temporal and, relatively speaking, within God (see below).

24. In this presentation of the doctrine of the trinity the following points are worthy of note:

1) the peculiar synthesis of economic and immanent aspects of the trinity that the concept of potency makes possible;

2) the conquest of the opposition of the immanence and transcendence of God by emphasizing the unity of cosmic and trinitarian events without weakening the transcendence of the divine self;

3) the joining of an empirical (economic trinity) and a speculative (immanent trinity) element based upon the character of the positive philosophy;

4) the founding of the triad in a three-fold act of will, cf. Thomasius, 1:105: "There are three absolute acts of will by virtue of which God . . . posits himself . . . threefold, and just because they are acts of will they establish a real distinction";

5) the affinity with the kenotic formula which, e.g., according to Hofmann, must be shown to be directly dependent upon the trinitarian construction, cf. *Schriftbeweis,* Lehrgang 2: 1: "The trinity that has become unequal to

itself has posited along with its first act of self-manifestation the beginning of the historical realization of the eternal will of God."

25. The unconditioned perfection of the natural process in man, man's, as it were, absoluteness in relation to natural beings, is derived from his consciousness, and is a consequence of his freedom—freedom from both principles that are operative in the process of nature—not only to transcend nature but to oppose it. Without a natural-philosophical construction of absolute being, a historical-philosophical construction would be impossible (see below).

26. The concept of the spirit world is highly characteristic of the relationship of the second and third potencies. So long as Schelling did not differentiate between them, nature was opposed to history as a real course of events to an ideal, and the concept of the spirit world did not exist. But when the third potency emerged as distinct and history was derived from the Fall, the second potency attained the significance of the spiritual and was used to construct a world of sub-spiritual beings with a preponderence of ideality and as a basis for the immortality of the soul.

27. Schelling discovered the unifying point of Kant's theoretical and practical philosophy in the original autonomy of the human spirit (see above). On the basis of his system of identity he discerned subjectivism in Fichte's conception of this principle and called the ego that posits itself the principle of original sin. Therefore, in the irrational moment of Kant's two critiques he succeeded in finding a point of unity that was opposed to the earlier one: the autonomy of the human ego is not reason, but opposed to reason. Intelligible freedom is the self-positing of the individual ego, and, inasmuch as it is individual, it is radical evil. Moreover, the world of the theoretical ego, which is included within space, time, and the categories, is posited by it in opposition to the true reality that is beyond this space, and this time, and these categories. Kant's critique has religious significance because it has revealed the subjective and therefore sinful development of the phenomenal world.

28. Schelling's Satanology is connected to this doctrine. For him, Satan is the will of the ground that has been actualized by the Fall and whose character is ambiguous. So far as he exists, he is what ought not to be; so far as he does not exist, he is the basis of all being. Besides these remarks, Schelling's Satanology, which reminds one of Goethe's characterization of Mephistophiles, can be passed over here, for it is only a concrete expression of the unitary will of the irrational ground and has had no influence on Schelling's construction of the history of religion.

Part II

1. The account of Schelling's construction of the history of religion given in this section is meant to provide a concrete basis and demonstration of the development of basic concepts given in the third section. Its purpose is not essentially in itself. This is especially the case with the section on mythology, whose empirical

material has been almost entirely superseded by modern research, although even here there is an abundance of ingenious and profound observations upon which, as Pfleiderer has correctly remarked, many learned poor could feast. Moreover, Schelling's construction is more vital and richer than Hegel's, which is usually considered the archetype of schemas of the history of religion and also is usually rejected. Schelling's voluntarism is more appropriate to the complex historical manifold of religions than are Hegel's logical categories.

2. Cf. Hofmann, *Schriftbeweis*, Lehrgang 4: 4: "Thus an event must occur by which the family of man is divided into a multitude of nations."

3. On more than one occasion Schelling used the doctrine of *Maya*, whose nature he discerned in the ambiguous character of the first potency to explain his doctrine of the dissimulation of the potencies in the creation. This is an important example of the romantic estimate and high regard for Indian Idealism; (it is important also for a determination of the relationship of romanticism and pessimism).

4. Cf. below the distinction between formal and material gods.

5. Here the ethical basis of Schelling's construction of the concept of God is made perfectly clear: God's righteousness is identical with his universality.

6. Cf. Hofmann, *Schriftbeweis*, Lehrgang 5: 6: "Now according to his calling Jesus must strive against all the effects of the will that is opposed to God, therefore also against the contradiction that it has caused until this will has become fully exhausted. Therefore he must strive until death."

7. On this view of the Reformation in its relationship to Catholicism and the Enlightenment, cf. Troeltsch, *Kultur der Gegenwart.*

Part III

1. As the history of Idealism has clearly shown, the formal critical method allows only three possibilities for a definition of religion, which correspond to the three Kantian critiques. The first possibility to be realized was inaugurated by Kant and was adopted by Fichte, and by Schelling in the earliest stages of his development with certain modifications pointed out above. It is the possibility of joining morality and religion. The second possibility was taken up by Schleiermacher in his *Reden.* He defines the essence of religion as the intuition of the infinite in the finite. He bases religion upon the aesthetic principle (cf. Windelband, *Lehrbuch der Geschichte der Philosophie*, 3d ed., p. 500). Schleiermacher's *Glaubenslehre* leads us no further (cf. n. 5., Part I, above). The third possibility is realized by Hegel, to be sure with important limitations. Like the later Schelling, his method is speculative. "Religion is the relationship of spirit to the absolute spirit" (*Religions philosophie*, 2d ed., 1: 200). However, this substantial relationship only becomes religion by being realized in the development of consciousness. There is no immediate intellectual intuition; elevation to the universal has to take

place in thought. "Religion is only through thought and in thought. God is not the highest experience, but the highest thought" (*ibid.*, p. 62). Thus the Kantian method produced an ethical, aesthetic, and intellectual concept of religion. They were in sharp conflict with one another, and in part still are. Herein lies the critique of this method.

2. This is undoubtedly circular. However, it is no reproach but a proof of the systematic perfection of the system. For it is the great insight of Fichte and the young Schelling that the unconditioned [*das Unbedingte*], which is the principle of the system, is nothing but freedom, the free act that posits itself as beginning.

3. The formal aprioristic method does not take the concept of God into consideration when constructing its concept of religion. Consequently it makes the former dependent upon the latter: God is the moral world order, or the causality of the feeling of dependence, or the absolute idea. God is not only formally—that is unavoidable—but also in terms of content the correlate of God-consciousness. He is, as Schelling formulated it, bound to the idea. What is lacking is the notion of power, in the face of which the will becomes obedient, feeling fearful, and thought attentive. The "that" in God is lacking, for which only a positive philosophy is adequate. To be sure, there can be no absolute antithesis here, for the law of identity requires that everything that is must also be related to the idea. This is the goal of philosophical religion. However, being has priority: God is the Lord.

4. The question can be raised to what extent this method differs from the theological method, since both begin with a given religion as absolute. The difference between them is not in terms of form but in terms of content. Whereas the theological method places a specific religion in deliberate and exclusive opposition to all others, it is precisely the essence of philosophical religion, on the basis of a specific religion, to adopt an attitude that is free from this religion as well as from all others. To be sure, this freedom must be required from everyone who wants to understand religion. Freedom is the unconditioned, the beginning of the system and its highest goal.

5. Therefore, apologetics is from the very start set on a false basis. It admits to its opponent that religion is the problem, instead of asking how irreligion or false religion is possible. Hence it also overlooks the importance of the interpretation of mythology and begins with the irreligious condition that prevailed at the end of the mythological process.

6. According to Schelling, revelation is not only the consequence but also the presupposition of mythology. Without the mediating potency "all human consciousness would be consumed and would cease to be human." "But why does the mediating potency remain in consciousness?" "It is not necessary that human consciousness should assert itself by going its own way and not be destroyed. This can only be the work of a free will." "Mythology is indeed the consequence, but it is in no way the special revelation of that divine decree [that human consciousness should not be lost]. This divine decree transcends mythology and is therefore only manifest for the first time in that which follows paganism in the order of time" (14: 8f.).

7. There is a very close correlation here with Schelling's philosophy of nature, in which likewise a sharp distinction is made between the product of nature, with which consciousness generally and empiricism are satisfied, and the creative and productive natural process—which has become inert in the product—in whose workshop true natural knowledge is immersed, observing and copying: this is the task of the philosophy of nature. Just as Schelling argued against those who would refute his deification of nature that they had no justification to presuppose a godless concept of nature, so also in the philosophy of mythology he struggles against those who presuppose an original atheistic consciousness and who with the aid of general psychological constructions look for the beginning of religions in an idolatrous deification of nature. A theory of nature that excludes God corresponds to an atheistic interpretation of religion. Schelling opposed both with the idealistic postulate that the truth of phenomena must be sought not in the product but in what produces it.

8. Enlightenment and Idealism, i.e., subjective idealism and objective idealism, are related to each other as reflection and mysticism. Therefore, mysticism can be called objective rationalism, because in it subject and object as such disappear in the unity of the intuition of reason. On the other hand, the arbitrary reflection and reasoning of the Enlightenment represent a thoroughly subjective use of reason. A thoroughly reasoned religion has been destroyed by Idealism by the demand of the dialectical method to become one with its object. Rational religion in the purest sense was conceived as mysticism, and therefore it was overcome.

9. Schelling allows the same judgment to fall in part upon his system of identity, since he identifies it expressly with the νόησις νοήσεως of Aristotle: "It seems incomprehensible that the negative character of this definition was overlooked in Aristotle's philosophy as well as in recent philosophy" (11: 559n). This agrees with Schelling's view that rationalism is an autonomous form of the Aristotelian substructure of orthodox theology. On the other hand, this does not appear to be in agreement with his view that Idealism has set consciousness free from pagan-rationalistic bondage. To be sure, within Idealism, Schelling distinguishes between negative and positive philosophy, and this view of Idealism applies properly to the latter. However, on account of its construction of the concept of autonomy, negative philosophy is the necessary presupposition of positive philosophy. The concept of autonomy, when properly understood, is the seed of the principle of positive philosophy, namely, freedom.

10. For evidence of the same idea in orthodoxy, cf. Troeltsch, *Vernunft und Offenbarung.*

11. Schelling attaches great importance to the fact that, in his construction, the foundation upon which revelation arises is not only rational religion, but also natural religion, i.e., mythology. The rationalist critique of revelation plays a winning game as long as it opposes revealed religion as the only form of actual religion. But now a principle of religion has been found that is independent of revelation, which is natural but not rational, so that the reality of the principle of revelation has been realized apart from its rational principle.

NOTES

169

12. The supernatural is spirit, spirit in a specific sense. For there is also a cosmic spirit that was realized, for example, at the end of paganism. This latter spirit was the consequence of a necessary process and was therefore unfree. But Spirit is supernatural inasmuch as it is free from its being-as-spirit, inasmuch as it is the absolute, exuberant freedom who remains lord even in the tension of the potencies and who is revealed in them. If Spirit were not free even from its being-as-spirit, then it would be bound to the world process. Then the concept of a free revelation would be impossible and God would be bound to the idea.

13. It now becomes clear in what sense Schelling can be called an irrationalist: in the sense of his assertion that everything that is, is related to the idea, but that in this relationship primacy belongs to being. This is represented concretely in the doctrine of the elevation of the irrational principle with the creation and the Fall. For, on account of this, the will has abandoned its original relationship to the idea: reality is irrational, the unity of the manifold in the idea has been lost and can only be perceived in mystical experience. Irrationalism is overcome in principle by the antithetical, irrational fact of revelation, and the world has become understandable.

14. The perfection of thought and that of action are equated by the act of the divine paradox: action is perfected in principle when, in the voluntary affirmation of the cross of Christ, the will sacrifices its own self that it posited outside God; thought perfects itself when in the thoughtful affirmation of the cross of Christ the dialectical process supersedes [aufheben] itself. The possibility for this kind of parallel consideration lies in the essence of the dialectical method, which is not subjective reflection about an object but an active rehearsal of the real process itself. The possibility of positing in principle an end of this process resides in Schelling's conception of the negative principle: wherever that which ought not to be is disclosed and made manifest in its entire depth as the absolute No, there further progress becomes impossible, for all progress proceeds through the No.

15. Schelling's philosophical religion is comparable to Hegel's doctrine that religion has the truth but not in the form of truth, and that therefore representation must be raised to thought. In his critique of the Hegelian doctrine, Schelling has clearly expressed the difference between himself and Hegel: "Pure thought, in which everything develops necessarily, knows nothing about a decision or an action or even a deed" (13: 173). Such categories pertain to representation. However, it is precisely on these that the philosophy of religion rests, and without them one would only reach a God who is the goal, the result of pure thought, who is therefore an idea of reason and not a God who is God in actuality, "who is the creator, who can begin something, who above all exists" (ibid., 172). "Being that precedes all thought is . . . that which is represented absolutely [das absolut Vorgestellte]" (Ibid., p. 173).

16. With the aid of his doctrine of qualitative times, Schelling attempted to solve the antinomy of time: present time has its limit in a qualitatively other, transcendent time. The same can be applied to the limitation of space.

17. By means of this concept of the doctrine of the intelligible Fall, history is

not debased; rather, its full significance is recognized. However, the concept of the Fall involves a change that leads it beyond its negative meaning. Schelling asked himself the question how a perversion within time can be united with the intelligible Fall. His answer was that "just allowing the good or evil principle to act in him is a consequence of the intelligible act" whereby the essence and life of a man are determined (7: 389).

18. The argument that the philosophy of nature drove him ultimately toward the positive philosophy appears questionable when one takes Hegel's philosophy of nature into consideration. However, Schelling rightly called Hegel's philosophy of nature an unmotivated positive element in Hegel's system. It is a foreign body in this purely teleological vision of the world. For once the question of the cause of the existing world is rejected, and its reality is interpreted only in terms of its goal, i.e., in terms of absolute self-consciousness (or Fichte's self-positing of the ego), then nature becomes only a means for a moral or generally spiritual self-conception. It ceases to represent an autonomous, separate realm on which a demand can be made that it be a goal. Only such a notion can give to the philosophy of nature the importance that it has for Schelling and its own validity. This also provides it with the power to break through the rational system generally. For the existence of nature remains incomprehensible unless it is interpreted aetiologically by means of an irrational principle.

19. Here indeed there seems to be some uncertainty in Schelling's construction, inasmuch as he literally identifies the cultural or rational with something that arises on pagan ground, and he abruptly rejects the claim of Romanticism to have, among other things, created Christian art. On the other hand, Schelling perceived in Idealism the principle of a Christian world consciousness, namely, that freedom which is independent of every external authority, even rational authority. But the latter is the only consistent viewpoint, especially if the opposition of natural and historical periods within history is emphasized. For this opposition has significance not only for God-consciousness but also for world-consciousness which, especially in Schelling's philosophy, are not to be separated. In this case, Idealism would inagurate philosophical religion only so long as it was instrumental in preserving for the cultural development its autonomous yet nevertheless specifically Christian principle. The realization of philosophical religion would occur at the end of the Christian historical period, just as the overcoming of natural religion occurred at the end of the pagan period. But whereas the rational process leads, on the basis of false religion, to catastrophe, the historical process during the Christian period succeeds to the consummation of religion. Nevertheless, Schelling only hinted at these ideas, and in part problematically.

20. As an example of a completed science, Schelling cites rational philosophy: by this he meant that science, brought to completion by him, whose goal is revelation. This applies to it because it is in fact complete. But it would be entirely different if an autonomous rational process were to develop on Christian ground. Such a process would occur only at the conclusion of this entire period, when it reached its goal. Since something like this is doubtless consistent with Schelling's

view of Idealism, it can be said that Schelling's irrationalism is directly opposed to Hegel's claim to have attained the end of the rational process.

21. This is not without difficulty, because the whole of actual history from its origin in transcendence has only the meaning of a moment within transcendent history. Nevertheless, Schelling suggested a solution when he interpreted the will of the logos to follow God-estranged being as a unitary will that has been effective in mythology and has become manifest in revelation. This unitary divine will, which is opposed to the will of the Fall, is therefore realized in history in successive stages, just as the will of man who comprehends himself. It belongs to the redemptive work of the logos to enter actual history and to forsake the ideal after man has renounced the idea. Will and counter-will constitute a moment from the viewpoint of transcendence.

22. When Kähler defines the supra-historical as "the living bond of that which remains universally valid with the historical in a dynamic present" (*Wissenschaft d. chr. Lehre*, 1: 19), his concept of that which remains universally valid makes the homogeneity of the conception of the "supra-historical" problematic for himself as well as for Schelling, for according to Schelling, the transcendent moves in precisely a supra-historical history. In his concept of the supra-historical, Kähler has formulated the problem of the indissolubility of the universally valid and the empirically historical. Schelling's conception of the supra-historical is an attempt to solve the problem by means of a doctrine of ideas applied to history. However, Kähler does not seem to have rejected the concept of a trinitarian history, for such a history is presupposed in some form whenever one speaks of a "tension" between the divine persons, as Kähler does. It is therefore natural that nothing is said of the manner in which this history is represented.

23. History is the necessary consequence of different acts of the divine will. Therefore, as soon as the category of will is predicated of the personal, triune life of God, a distinction between potential and actual trinity is unavoidable in some form.

24. But then it should be noted that popular reproaches accusing Schelling of pantheism or monism are not applicable here. Schelling's attitude toward pantheism has been stated above. Schelling's position with regard to monism is as follows: He admits 1) an aetiological monism: the ideal world is the perfect expression of the divine nature, and therefore it is the basis of his personality; 2) a teleological monism: in the world as it should be, God is all in all; his nature is in conscious unity with his self; 3) an empirical dualism: the world as it is is determined by an anti-divine principle.

25. Schelling is a nominalist insofar as he gives priority to the absolute individual, to the primordial "that." The infinite idea has reality only because it is the absolute individual. However, he is also a thorough-going realist because he maintains that the principles of being, in which God has placed his will, comprise what is actually real in all events and because he regards the particular products of the natural and historical process as only conditioned reality.

26. Even this mode of expression is already mythologized. With respect to the

temptation, Schelling can in principle speak only of that supra-historical decision whereby the second potency resolved to follow God-estranged being into suffering and death. The renunciation by the second potency of the sovereignty that it achieved during the pagan period is a moment of realization of the divine will.

27. Kuno Fischer's opinion is similar to this. However, he has not taken into consideration the development of Schelling's thought from the *Lectures on the Method of Academic Study* to the positive philosophy.

TRANSLATOR'S NOTES

i. During this century, Schelling scholarship has made considerable progress, especially with respect to the interpretation of Schelling's late philosophy. Its foundations were laid by Manfred Schröter, whose dissertation, *Der Ausgangpunkt der Metaphysik Schellings*, was presented to the University of Jena in 1908. Schröter's edition of Schelling's works (*Schellings Werke nach der Originalausgabe in neuer Anordnung*, Munich, 1927–59, 12 vols.) is a rearrangement of the works included in the standard edition edited by Schelling's son, K. F. A. Schelling (1856–61). Schröter's arrangement is intended to facilitate interpretation of Schelling's development, and is especially useful for the late period. Schröter planned to edit additional volumes from the *Nachlass* containing materials not included in the standard edition, which would enable scholars to reconstruct the progress of Schelling's thought from 1809, when he published his last major work (*On the Nature of Human Freedom*), until 1841–45, when Schelling lectured in Berlin on the philosophy of mythology and revelation. Unfortunately, most of this material was destroyed by bombing during World War II. Only one *Nachlassband* has appeared, containing two early versions of Schelling's unfinished work *Die Weltalter* (*Die Weltalter, Fragmente, in der Urfassungen von 1811 und 1813*, Munich, 1946); this volume includes a long introduction by Schröter. Horst Fuhrmans's edition of Schelling's Erlangen lecture from a student transcript (F. W. J. Schelling, *Initia Philosophiae Universae, Erlanger Vorlesung, WS 1820/21*, Bonn, 1969) with an interpretive essay and voluminous notes is another valuable contribution to the study of this interim period. Fuhrmans is also editing Schelling's letters and documents (F. W. J. Schelling, *Briefe und Dokumente*, Bonn, 1962–), of which two volumes have so far appeared. Almost all of Schröter's writings about Schelling, including his dissertation, have been published in *Kritische Studien über Schelling und zur Kulturphilosophie* (Munich, 1971). The *Festgabe* presented to Schröter on his 85th birthday (*Schellingstudien*, Munich, 1965) contains two essays that relate especially to the themes of Tillich's dissertations: Horst Fuhrmans, *Der Gottesbegriff der Schellingschen positiven Philosophie*, and Louis van Bladel, *Die Funktion der Abfallslehre in der Gesamtbewegung der Schellingschen Philosophie*. See also Fuhrmans's two studies: *Schellings letzte Philosophie, die negative und positive Philosophie im Einsatz des Spätidealismus* (Berlin, 1940), and *Schellings Philosophie der Weltalter* (Düsseldorf, 1954). Walter Schulz's *Die Vollendung des deutschen Idealismus in der Spätphilosophie Schellings* (Stuttgart, 1955) deserves mention here as a recent influential study. Schelling's theory of myth receives favorable treatment from Ernst Cassirer in the second volume of his *Philosophy of Symbolic Forms* (New Haven, Conn., 1955); Martin Heidegger's views of Schelling have been recently published in *Schellings Abhandlung über das Wesen der menschlichen Freiheit* (Tübingen, 1971): this volume contains the text of a lecture given by Heidegger on Schelling in 1936 and selections from manuscripts containing commentary on Schelling's *On the Nature of Human Freedom*, which Heidegger had prepared in anticipation of a seminar on Schelling to be given in 1941. Neither Cassirer's nor Heidegger's works are in the main line of Schelling scholarship, but for obvious reasons they are of great interest and are therefore mentioned here. Finally, Guido Schneeberger's, *Friedrich Wilhelm Joseph Schelling, eine Bibliographie*, lists items by and about Schelling through 1953.

ii. Kuno Fischer, *Geschichte der neuern Philosophie*, Vol. 6, Book I, *Schellings Leben und Schriften*, Book II, *Schellings Lehre*, 2d ed. (Heidelberg, 1895). Notwithstanding Tillich's criticism, Fischer's work remains even today a valuable source of information.

iii. For bibliographical details on pertinent works by these authors, see Schneeberger's bibliography (cited above, n. i).

iv. The distinction is between *Wille (voluntas)* and *Willkür (arbitrium)*. The former is the legislative power of the will, the power of the will to posit ends and to formulate maxims; it is translated throughout as "will." The latter is the faculty of choice between alternatives, and is translated throughout as "choice," "arbitrary choice", or as arbitrariness. For a discussion of the concepts of *Wille* and *Willkür* in Kant, cf. John R. Silber's introduction to the English translation of Kant's *Religion within the Limits of Reason Alone* (New York, 1960), pp. xxivff.

v. "The opposition of equally possible acts in consciousness is, therefore, the sole condition by which the absolute act of will can become anew an object of the ego. However, this opposition is precisely that which transforms the absolute will [*Wille*] into choice [*Willkür*]. Hence, choice is the appearance sought by us of the absolute will, but not the original act itself of will. The absolute act of freedom with which all consciousness begins now becomes an object" (SW, 3: 576). This original act of will is, of course, the self-positing act of the absolute ego, which is the fundamental principle of Fichte's system, which Schelling made his own. But in Schelling's development, particularly in its last phase, it undergoes an important transformation. In the thought of the later Schelling, this primary act of will is viewed as an irrational act, and is reinterpreted as the principle of sin. For a discussion of the principle in Fichte's system, cf. Heath and Lachs, trans., *Fichte: Science of Knowledge with First and Second Introductions* (New York, 1970), preface, pp. xiiiff.

vi. *Übergewicht*, i.e., predominance, is an important term in Schelling's doctrine of the potencies. A potency is a union of the subjective and the objective principle, of the real and the ideal in which one or the other predominates or is quantitatively greater. In Schelling's later philosophy the potencies are represented as conflicting wills.

vii. The periods of Schelling's development thus far mentioned are first, his Fichtean period; second, the "philosophy of nature," in which Schelling endeavored to present nature as an egolike process and not as the mere limiting principle that the ego posits for itself (as Fichte conceived it). During the third period of his development, Schelling formulated his "system of identity," in particular, in his work *Darstellung meines Systems der Philosophie* [*Exposition of My System of Philosophy*] (SW 4: 105–212), published in 1801; here he united both preceding points of view, transcendental idealism and philosophy of nature, in a system of idealrealism founded upon the principle of identity.

viii. In 1802, the year following the publication of his *Darstellung meines Systems der Philosophie*, Schelling published his dialogue *Bruno*, subtitled "Concerning the Divine and Natural Principle of Things," and delivered his *Vorlesungen über die Methode des akademischen Studiums* [Lectures on the Methods of Academic Study]. In both works he presents his doctrine of ideas in the context of the system of identity.

ix. *Philosophische Untersuchungen über das Wesen der menschlichen Freiheit die damit zusammenhängenden Gegenstände* [Philosophical Investigations on the Nature of Human Freedom and Themes Related to It]. Here and elsewhere I refer to this work by its short title.

x. κατ᾽ ἐξοχήν, i.e., par excellence, *sensu eminenti*.

xi. In distinguishing between μὴ ὄν and οὐκ ὄν, Schelling notes that, in Greek, the negative μὴ is used in modal, in particular, imperative, statements, whereas, οὐκ is used in indicative statements. Hence μὴ ὄν is modal nonbeing; it is what can be, but is not, or what is, but should not be. Οὐκ ὄν is what is not pure and simple. In the system of the potencies, modal nonbeing is the first potency. It is the real principle, the real basis of the personality, irrational freedom that contradicts the rational will. Although it is the necessary basis of life, it must be surpassed dialectically.

xii. *Das sein Sollende* is translated here as both "what ought to be and shall be." It is the goal or purpose of becoming, Aristotle's final cause, the third potency. On the dual meaning of *sollen,* cf. Ellen Bliss Talbot, *The Fundamental Principle of Fichte's Philosophy,* Cornell Studies in Philosophy, no. 7 (New York, 1906) pp. 112f.

xiii. On the concept of nature in God, cf. Kurt Leese, *Von Jakob Böhme zu Schelling, Zur Metaphysik des Gottesproblems* (Erfurt, 1927).

xiv. On the distinction between material and formal freedom, Tillich's second Schelling dissertation Part I, II, 2. See also Schelling, *On the Nature of Human Freedom,* SW 7: 351ff. and 383ff. It should be noted that what Tillich calls "material freedom," Schelling calls "ideal" or "formal" freedom: what Tillich calls "formal freedom," Schelling calls "real" or "vital" freedom.

xv. In *On the Nature of Human Freedom,* Schelling does not say that "the stages of the world process are the stages by which [God] becomes personal and conscious," or that "God becomes self-conscious and spirit" in man. What he does say is that the world, and man, its center, are necessary for God's self-revelation. But it is a moral and not a logical and metaphysical necessity that governs the divine choice to create the world. Moral necessity, far from being incompatible with freedom and consciousness, presupposes them. To be sure, when moral necessity is attributed to God, it becomes metaphysical necessity also, because God is the source of all that is. Moral necessity leads to a goal that is the *telos* of the historical process. This *telos* is God, who will be all in all, the goal of Pauline mysticism (cf. 1 Cor. 15:28). Thus, there is a difference between God before and after creation, but it is a difference between the decision of love and fulfillment. Cf. SW 7: 373ff. and 394ff. Cf. also Tillich, *Systematic Theology,* 3: 394–423.

xvi. Schelling quotes Kant's *Critique of Pure Reason,* A 613, B 641.

xvii. Schelling here quotes Newton's *Principia,* the general scholium at the conclusion of Book III. There Newton makes a distinction between God as world soul and God as lord of the world and contends that only the latter is a correct concept of God. "This being governs all things, not as the soul of the world, but as Lord over all; and on account of his dominion he is wont to be called Lord God, παντοκράτωρ, or *Universal Ruler;* for *God* is a relative word, and has respect to servants; and Deity is the dominion of God not over his own body, as those imagine who fancy God to be the soul of the world, but over servants." Quoted by Alexandre Koyre, *From the Closed World to the Infinite Universe,* (Baltimore, Md., 1957), p. 225. Cf. also Schelling's distinction between cosmic and divine spirit.

xviii. Hegel, *Encyclopedia,* second part, *Philosophy of Nature,* §§ 248–50.

xix. Before the Fall, the world exists beside *(praeter)* God, distinct from him, but in immediate relation to him; after the Fall, the world exists outside *(extra)* God, in estrangement from him; things within the fallen world are substantially empty *(Gehaltlos)*, i.e., they can die or be destroyed. The fallen world is related to God through the mediation of the potencies (which in their separateness mark the ages of world history); this mediated relationship is realized in human institutions, specifically, religion and the state; religion discloses the inner meaning of history, the state represents history's outer meaning. This relationship, however, remains unfulfilled so long as it remains within the limits of what is *(das Seiende)*, so long as it is mediated by the potencies; it remains unfulfilled until that which is beyond being *(das Überseiende)* is revealed as God, the lord of being, who will be "All in All."

xx. Zabism: Schelling may have been referring to the astral religion of the Sabaeans, a people occupying the kingdom of Saba, in southwest Arabia during pre-Islamic times.

xxi. For the relation of religion and culture, cf. Tillich's *Philosophy of Religion,* esp. Part I, English trans. in *What is Religion?* (New York, 1969), pp. 56–101. Tillich's method of correlation is based upon this relationship between religion and philosophy, between the mythological and the rational process.

xxii. νόησις νοήσεως, i.e., the intelligence of intellect: ". . . a divine mind knows itself, since it is the supreme excellence, and its intelligence is the intelligence of intellect." Aristotle, *Metaphysics,* 1074b 34 (Hope translation).

xxiii. ἄπρακτος τάς ᾽εξω πράξεις, he who is inactive with respect to external actions: Schelling's reference is to Aristotle's unmoved mover, as the God of purely rational philosophy. I have been unable to find this expression in Aristotle's works.

xxiv. κρεῖττον τοῦ λογόυ, greater than reason: Schelling's reference here is to Aristotle's *Eudemian Ethics,* 1248a 27ff: "The object of our search is this—what is the commencement of movement in the soul? The answer is clear: as in the universe, so in the soul, God moves everything. For in a sense the divine element in us moves everything. The starting-point of reasoning is not reasoning, but something greater. What, then, could be greater even than knowledge and intellect but God?" (Oxford translation.)

xxv. This demand is the theme of Tillich's second Schelling dissertation.

xxvi. "The idea of the trinity passes through three moments: it must proceed from *tautousia,* where only the Father is the dominating *ousia*—where the Father comprehends all; it must proceed from *tautousia* through *heteroousia,* which lasts as long as there is tension [between the potencies] until the final reconciliation, to *homoousia,* which, therefore, is only the final moment, which is totally incomprehensible apart from the two that precede it" (SW 14: 66). *Homoousia,* the communion of the Father and the Son in the Holy Spirit, is the goal of history.

xxvii. *Philosophie der Offenbarung, drittes Buch, sechsunddreissigste Vorlesung,* SW 14: 294ff.

xxviii. *Einleitung in die Philosophie der Mythologie, zweites Buch: Philosophische Einleitung in die Philosophie der Mythologie oder Darstellung der reinrationalen Philosophie,* SW 11. Tillich is referring to the first lecture (numbered eleven). This work is Schelling's latest and most authoritative exposition of his "negative philosophy."

xxix. Because the potencies are conceived in spiritual personality (in universal man, or God) in perfect harmony, i.e., in their complete realization, they are no longer called *potencies* but *principles.* They have been negated and reaffirmed in that which is absolutely nonpotent. Cf. SW 8: 309.

xxx. Tillich is referring here to Schelling's *Historisch-kritische Einleitung in die Philosophie der Mythologie,* SW 11.

xxxi. On the reversal of the meaning of subject and object, cf. Tillich's n. 9 to Part I of the present work.

INDEX

179